Treasures
Hidden in the Darkness

by

Carole Logsdon
with Dan Wooding

Promise Publishing Co. Santa Ana CA 92711

Treasures Hidden in the Darkness

Published by Promise Publishing Co.
Santa Ana CA 92711
United States of America

Scripture quotations used by permission.

Logsdon, Carole

Treasures Hidden in the Darkness

ISBN 0-939497-58-1

"I will go before you,
and level the mountains
And smash down the city gates
of brass and iron bars.

And I will give you

***treasures hidden in the darkness**,*

secret riches;

and you will know that I am doing this—

I,

the Lord God of Israel,
the one Who calls you by your name."

Isa.45: 2-3

Dedicated to

Juanita S. Reynolds

My Mother, My Life Friend

Acknowledgements

To Dr. Lee and Gloria Bendell who saw the potential for this book and gave of their time to encourage me and to pray. Thank you for your presence within minutes after Duane went home to be with the Lord. Your love and strength meant so much.

To Dr. Clyde and Ruth Narramore, Narramore Christian Foundation, thank you for your counselling and encouragement to write. To Ruth for publishing my first article in the Psychology for Living magazine on the Divorce of Adult Children. To Dr. Clyde for writing the foreword to this book and believing in me. This gave me courage to start out on a bigger project.

To Dan Wooding and his wife, Norma. To Dan for taking the rough manuscript and developing it. To Norma for her honest evaluations from a personal point of view.

To Dr. Ed Nederland, a big thank you for taking your time to listen to the Scriptures and the direction the Lord seemed to be giving. Also for your encouragement, spiritual and business counsel. Also, thank you for giving me the opportunity to minister to others.

To Dr. Darrell and Marion Countryman who gave of their time and love to send faxes every day for several years during Duane's long illness and after his death. The daily faxes gave us courage and strength to carry on. Thank you both for your prayers, encouragement and willingness to be a burden-bearer in our time of need.

To Bonnie Morris, my friend, prayer partner and burden-bearer. Thank you for being my aide, freeing my time to write. You have worn many hats which made this book possible.

To the Reverend Argie and Pat Blackburn, thank you for your faithful friendship, for your inspiration and encouragement to keep on keeping on.

To Dr. Earl Henslin, friend, counselor and one who walked with us so faithfully through Duane's illness and homegoing and for months afterward.

To Dr. Paul Ovando, Duane's surgeon, and Chris, his surgical nurse, thank you for your compassion and loving care during our hardest hours of pain.

To Dr. Patricia Tretter and the staff of St. Jude Hospital, thank you for the specialized love and care you give.

To the many people who have prayed so faithfully in their Bible Study Groups during our times of grief and through the completion of this book, thank you all for your faithful support in prayer and for your notes of encouragement. Without you, this project would not be a reality.

To pastors, Buck Buchanan and John Coulombe of the Evangelical Free Church of Fullerton, California for giving support and for offering opportunities to minister to others who hurt. Thank you for Duane's Celebration of Life service and for being such a comfort to our family.

Last and not least, thank you to my friend and editor, Mary Belle Steele, whose work, counsel and wisdom transformed the manuscript for publication.

Foreword

What should you do when things do not turn out well?

What's the best way to handle problems that are right in the center of your family? Worse still, what if you are a committed Christian and, in fact, a Christian leader?

Should you keep things quiet? Or should you deny what's going on, hoping they'll get better? Should you tell someone—or is there anyone in whom you can confide? If others hear about it, what will they say, and how will they treat you? Even worse, how will it affect the cause of Christ? Should you take the sickly route of reluctantly blaming yourself even though you've done the best you could and have followed the teachings of the Scripture?

What about the disappointed and angry feelings you have toward your grown children? And the "in-laws"? Will the secret feelings of anger toward God finally disappear? Will your family somehow have a testimony again?

These are questions which faced Carole Logsdon and her late husband, Duane. Added to all of the devastating problems which descended upon her family, was the mysterious, very serious and lingering illness and eventual death of her husband whom she loved so much.

As you read this book, I'm sure that like the rest of us, you'll identify with certain parts, but even more, you'll be amazed at Carole's insight, her dependence upon the Lord, her humanity, and what she decided to do.

How I wish we had more people like Carole.

Dr. Clyde Narramore

Foreword

In our world, when things break, they lose their value and we discard them. In God's economy, it is just the opposite—until there is brokenness, treasures remain hidden and unappreciated. According to Paul, pain and discomfort are some of the tools God uses to break our containers and reveal "His greatness, His power and His strength within"(II Corinthians 4:16-18).

The Apostle reminds us that the treasure ("Christ in you") is hidden until the clay pot is broken. Life has a way of throwing more at us than we feel we can endure: It beats us *up*, throws us *down*, crushes us *within* and almost takes us *out*—hitting us from every angle and direction! And in our brokenness, the light of God's grace and love is beamed to those around.

My friend, Carole Logsdon, gives us a glimpse of the painful and human side of her life and losses through multiple deaths and divorces, as well as disillusionment, depression and anger. She reveals from personal experience that good Christians do go through bad times, and when the **ideal** life becomes an **ordeal** and a **raw deal**, we are forced to deal with it, or run and hide. She dealt with it.

I encourage you to journey back with her through her life lessons, and explore the treasures that appear in your own dark experiences. I think you'll relate.

John Coulombe
Pastor, Senior Adult Ministries
Evangelical Free Church
Fullerton, California

Table of Contents

Poems

Table of Contents

An open letter to my dear Children:

We have a common history for over forty years. As someone has said, "A lot of water has gone under the bridge." There have been many joys, sorrows and tears. There have been circumstances that have challenged our relationships but I want to thank you, each one, for the love that you've given to your Dad and to me in our time of need. Thank you for being with us in our experiences of confinement, surgeries, death and many emotional changes. The respect, love and support that you gave were beautiful and your sacrifices did not go unnoticed.

THERE IS A PLACE OF THANKFULNESS

We have all experienced personal loss from different perspectives. This book is from my perspective as a mother, mother-in-law, and grandmother. I missed many of your joys and sorrows, no doubt, because of physical exhaustion, isolation, grief and the loneliness of widowhood. Thank you for being patient with me. Thank you for all of your calls home, just to talk or to see how things were going. Thank you for the visits where *time* was the gift so we could bond as adults and share our lives.

Thank you not only for sharing your joys but your hurts as well. This has given me the joy of praying for you and still feeling like a mom. Thank you for hearing and accepting apologies where Dad and I failed you as parents. Thank you for sharing your shortcomings and apologies as well. Thank you for being there when Dad and I needed you most.

THERE HAVE BEEN PLACES OF STRUGGLE

One of the hardest experiences in life is having to watch a loved one, your own flesh and blood, go through suffering or loss. This is such a helpless feeling. We have all reacted to this stress in different ways.

Another hard place in life is to suffer the guilt of not helping a loved one in the hours when they needed us most. This is a time which leaves scars. It takes a strong and loving family to understand and not to blame others. Often when we walk through a difficult experience, we see too late how we could have helped. Maturity doesn't come overnight regardless of age. It is important that we keep short accounts with each other. Life is too short to carry hurts with us.

THERE IS A PLACE OF CHOICE

Only God knows why individuals or families go through crises. I do know that we have a choice in how we handle each one. Since we are human beings with sinful natures, none of us is perfect.

When you boys were small, each of you accepted the Lord as your personal Savior. Being raised in a minister's home you witnessed friends and people of our congregations at their best as well as at their worst. Some of these crisis times could have caused you never to walk inside the door of another church—some have not "walked" their "talk." Some of you have watched the physical suffering and death of little ones that God has given you for just a few years. All of these experiences are enough for you to lose heart and not see the Lord as caring and loving.

Dad and I too have shared these seasons of life with you and we have hurt with you. We questioned, became angry and bewildered at the Lord's permitting experiences of this nature. Some of you, my grandchildren, have gone through the pain of a split family and you, too, have felt that God turned His back and didn't see your hurt. These are normal feelings; still, I've learned that just because I feel that way doesn't change God's love for me nor take away His presence. He has a reason for everything that happens in our life. There are some questions that we will not find the answers to this side of heaven.

Experiencing grief is not only a journey, it is a personal process of getting acquainted with new feelings, learning who we are and how we react. It is also a commitment, trusting the Lord and giving Him whatever time He needs to help us through the journey. Grief brings out a very deep emotional stress and we can be almost overwhelmed by the power of these waves of emotion.

> *Even when we are too weak to have any faith left, he remains faithful to us and will help us, for he cannot disown us who are part of himself, and he will always carry out his promises to us* (II Timothy 2:13).

The telling of these life experiences is only a part of my grief recovery process. If we are to have spiritual depth with God, we must not only talk truthfully to Him about our hurts and disappointments, we must also listen to what He tells us from His Word. The Bible is personal, living, powerful and life-changing. If we neglect God's Word, we have already lost the victory in our time of grief and we also lose an opportunity to grow in our spiritual maturity.

I thank the Lord for each one of you and the blessings that you have given me. Your Dad and I have always felt that we have a wonderful family and that each one of you is a gift from God. I feel the same about you, my new "daughters-in-love"—Renee, Jeri, Rosemary and Angie along with the seven new step-grandchildren.

It is my prayer that you will all seek Jesus, trust Him and live for Him in the days that you have before you.

Love,

Mom and Grandma

Chapter One

Family Life

OUR PRAYER

"My son, do not forget my law,
but let your heart keep my commands;
For length of days and long life and peace
they will add to you" (Proverbs 3:1,2-NKJ)

We dedicate our children to God
While in their infancy.
Actually, we dedicate ourselves
To raise them all successfully.

We teach and train and sacrifice
So they'll accept the Lord,
That they may grow in godliness
And walk in the light of His Word.

We have no way of forcing this,
So all we do is pray
That as they grow, become adults,
They will not go astray.

Sometimes in process of their growth,
They choose a different way
That leads to pain and sometimes tears -
A price we sometimes pay.

As parents, we persist in prayer
That our children feel the need
To walk with Him in fellowship.
For this we earnestly plead.

He will lead them step by step
As they walk with Him in love.
They'll know real peace and joy within -
Gifts from their Father above.

Duane D. Logsdon

Chapter 1

FAMILY LIFE

Why does the telephone always seem to ring at the most inconvenient time? My hands were sticky from rolling out homemade noodles for the dinner I was preparing for Doug (our youngest son) and Debbie, his wife. As I ran for the phone, I noticed the clock on the stove. It said 4 P.M.

"Mom, it's Debbie," she said. "I have bad news. Doug is in the hospital emergency room; he's been run over by a truck." Her words nearly made my heart stop! Debbie continued, "All I know is that he left about an hour ago, and for some reason, as I saw him leave, I had a funny feeling."

As the four boys grew up, Duane and I went through our share of cars, motorcycles, and camping incidents, but nothing like this had ever happened.

Duane and I left our home in Fullerton (Orange County, California) for Upland, a town nestled at the foot of the San Bernardino Mountains. We wanted to be with Debbie and her parents who were at the hospital with Doug. It seemed to take forever to drive the 30 miles or so. When we arrived, to our amazement, we saw Doug and Debbie walking out of the hospital. The doctors had released Doug to go home, telling him to come back if he had any problems. He still had the tire marks of the truck embedded in his back. The doctors had called all their staff into the emergency room, and any doctor that was available was asked to check this guy over. By rights he should have been dead; however, not even a broken bone nor any internal injuries showed up in the tests or X-rays.

Doug told us how he was hit and thrown under the tires of the truck. It was horrifying. He remembered yelling and pushing his chest off the cement with his arms. As the truck rolled over his back, his body seemed to move in ways over which he had no control. We all praised the Lord for this miracle. Even the paramedics and the police at the scene of the accident could not believe what they witnessed.

This was such an amazing miracle that in the months to come it helped to stabilize my faith in a loving God. I came to believe that if the Lord would do this, He could (and would) do anything else we needed.

Duane and I met at Mount Vernon Union High School in Mount Vernon, Washington when we were teenagers. Duane was "Yell King" for the Bulldogs football team and I was a cheerleader. We fell in love and were married on August 26, 1949 in the First Baptist Church of Mount Vernon. My grandfather even sold his prized dapple-gray workhorses to buy my wedding dress. As Duane placed the gold ring on the third finger of my left hand and we kissed, I knew that we were linked for life – "for better for worse, in sickness and in health," as we promised that day.

Since Duane and I were married very young, we literally grew up with our sons. Being an only child and raised in an adult world, I had many adjustments to make as a wife and a mother. It seemed the boys were always either on top of, or climbing underneath something, swinging from or jumping off things constantly. My continual prayer was, "Lord, help me to be a good Mom. Please give me patience ... and while You are at it, please keep these boys from killing each other or themselves." I was getting a little concerned about asking the Lord for "patience" because it seemed that every time I prayed that prayer we got another son and I was already inundated with trying to keep up with the boys we had.

Shortly after we placed our faith in Jesus Christ, Duane felt called of the Lord to study for the ministry. Duane studied at Bob Jones University in Greenville, South Carolina, and we lived in a shabby trailer park nicknamed "Tar Paper Shack Town." At that time, we had Don (2 years old) and David (13 months old). Three years later, in Duane's junior year, our third son, Daniel was born. The other boys already had him named so we had no choice in the matter. As far as they were concerned, this baby was going to be a boy and his name was going to be Daniel. It wasn't until six years later that our son Doug was born.

The boys delighted in stretching their Mother's patience and nervous system. One evening while starting a load of clothes in the washing machine, I put my hand in the machine to see if it was empty before turning on the water. Well, it wasn't empty! I almost went ballistic. One of the boys had put a live snake in there. Since snakes created such a response, they tried it again, this time coiling a dead rattlesnake, as it froze, in the big freezer in our garage. They put plastic bugs in the tossed salads (dinner guests or not), and they loved going grocery shopping with me. Arriving at the check stand, I would find chocolate covered ants and strange gourmet foods that made my stomach turn over. I have yet to find out who did what.

When meal times came around, we had anywhere from six to ten people at the table. Usually, at least one of the boys brought a friend. The boys helped their Dad in the mornings by working in the shop (Duane did plumbing work to support the family) and they helped me in the evenings. Our meals and cleanup times were a family routine. It was important to Duane and me that we eat meals together as a family. We caught up on the day's activities, and it was a time to share devotions and pray together. All the boys learned to cook, clean house and do their own washing. At times though, we all worried about Doug. There was a time when I had to choose between a relationship with him or a clean room. Today his house is probably cleaner than mine. I'm proud to watch the boys do these things now. It reminds me of how we worked together in our everyday life when they were at home.

The boys today are all different and have different interests. Don loves art, music and sports and he is a successful businessman. David is a gourmet cook, loves to work with his hands and as a second career, he is now a Doctor of Chiropractic. Dan is a businessman, and has his own business. He loves music and works in his church doing solos and working with singing groups. Doug also has his own business, loves sports and coaches junior young people in football and baseball. He also collects and rides motorcycles.

Today, we all have so much to be thankful for and I will never forget that, in the protection of the Lord, we raised the boys without any major tragedy. Duane captured our hopes and dreams in his poem, "Our Prayer," as he was to do so many times as the years passed. He seemed to express our deepest longings with his pen and paper—our faith, our treasures, our expectations.

"O Lord, what miracles you do!
And how deep are your thoughts."
Psalm 91:5 (TLB)

Chapter Two

Changed Life

TRUST

"Take no thought for tomorrow"-
that's commanded by our Lord.
It sounds simple when we read it,
But applying it is hard.

It's not that we don't love Him.
For He knows indeed we do.
Our problem, very simply put,
Is having faith He'll see us through.

We believe that He accepts us;
When we receive Him as our Lord.
But to trust that He'll take care of us
Is hard, though promised in His Word.

How do we deal with this problem
That's so real to all of us?
It's simple - yet it's really not-
For it requires implicit trust.

We must trust Him when we're healthy.
We must trust Him when we're ill.
We must trust Him to supply our needs.
With peace our hearts He'll fill.

Duane D. Logsdon

Chapter 2

CHANGED LIFE

<u>December 8, 1988</u>

The Christmas tree was up and decorated in our Fullerton home. As usual, Duane hung all the lights and tinsel then I added all the balls, bows and ornaments. We stood back, hand in hand, to take a look at our finished product. The old tree had served us well for about eight years, and we still loved it. There was something about the ritual of putting up our tree that had special meaning for us. Still, this year was different.

Without saying a word, we each knew what the other was thinking. Would this be the last time we would put up this tree together? Somehow that extra hug and kiss was deep and meaningful. That day, that hour, we were together and we were going to make the most of it regardless of the future. We knew that the Lord would supply His grace for each of us ... no matter what the future held.

<u>December 11, 1988</u>

The morning went by too fast. Our son, David, had come in from Washington State the day before. Our suitcases were packed for a ten-day stay at a hotel near St. Vincent Medical Center in Los Angeles. We were waiting for our son, Don, and Pennie, our daughter-in-law, from Riverside, California. Duane wanted to be sure the accommodations that he had arranged for us were adequate and he wanted to see that our things were settled in the hotel rooms before he checked into the hospital.

The week before we had kept an appointment with Dr. Ralph Nelson at the House Institute of Otology in Los Angeles for Duane's hearing problem. Somehow, we did not anticipate anything beyond a hearing loss and maybe a hearing aid to help his deficiency. We were not ready for the diagnosis ... an Acoustic Neuroma … a tumor within the inner ear. We were told that the surgical procedure would entail a craniotomy. The incision would be in front of the left ear and would curve behind the hair line to about three inches above the ear and down behind the ear. The tumor was to be reached through a window in the skull, lifting the brain and down into the inner ear.

We both were in a state of shock for several days. We were frightened; we prayed, cried, and searched the Scriptures for comfort and help; and we talked with our family. In the meantime, surgical preparations were being made by a team of four specialists.

December 12, 1988

On the morning of the surgery, I walked beside Duane into the surgical wing. When we arrived at the big double doors, the attendant said, "This is where we have to part. Have you received all your instructions about seeing the doctors after surgery?" I assured him that I had. At the same time, I gave Duane a kiss on his cheek. He already knew that Doug and Debbie were there, also Don, Pennie, Dan and David. He was aware (as I was) that many of our family and friends were praying hard for us at this hour.

Duane seemed very much at peace. I could not say the same for myself. We had both committed this to our Heavenly Father and only He knew the outcome. This was one of the hardest days of my life and, I might add, the longest. Putting Duane in the hands of the Lord was about to kill me. If this surgery went wrong, how could I live without him? It was 11:30 A.M.

We did not hear anything until 3:30 P.M. when the doctors arrived to say there had been complications in the surgeries ahead of Duane and they hadn't even started his operation yet. To say the least, we were very upset. My anxiety grew. Where had Duane been kept all this time and why were we not notified sooner of this delay?

It was 8:30 P.M. when the doctors finally told us that the surgery was over and that Duane had done very well. They were confident that his hearing would be restored even though they'd had to take the balance nerve. He would have to regain the ability to walk by sheer grit until the other side of the brain took over. He would be in Intensive Care for approximately two days and three nights.

For me, the day at the hospital was full of fear and uneasiness. Many times, I left the family in the waiting room and searched for a quiet corner in order to be alone, to pray and pour my heart out to the Lord. When one of the Sisters at the hospital checked on the family and saw that I was missing, she'd come looking for me. She held me while I cried and she prayed and tried to encourage me. This happened several times during that day. It seemed like she was a personal messenger from the Lord whom He sent to let me know that He cared and that He was standing with us in this trial. I will never forget her.

When we left to go back to the hotel, the only thing that seemed to comfort me were the hourly calls to ICU. Somehow, just holding my Bible in dazed sleep seemed to help. By this time I was too tired to pray. It all seemed like a dream and my emotions were numb and dull; I was unable to feel anything. Somehow, I sensed that *something wasn't right.*

December 22, 1988

For Duane, each day was filled with new victories, new strength and less pain. On the tenth day, Duane was discharged from the hospital to take the long trip home. The noise of the car and the traffic made him very ill. Once home, Pennie and I settled him in his bed; he seemed very weak and fragile but we were happy to get him home. This spoke to us of God's faithfulness. Having Duane with us was the only Christmas gift that any of us wanted. As a family, all the boys and their wives were supportive and caring - we felt very rich and blessed. We had each other; we had our family and the days ahead would be filled with progress and recovery. My own trust and hope though seemed to hang by a thread. I knew the Lord could heal Duane … but would He? I still could not say to the Lord, "Thy will be done."

January 8. 1989

We were still counting our blessings. Just being together was special. Our "BIG THING" at that time, was a trip to a local Carl's Jr. restaurant for a barbecued chicken sandwich, and a walk in the park. The day came when

Duane was able to walk solo in the park while I watched. It had been a long journey for him and I admired his bravery and perseverance to do what it took to get well and walk again without help.

But during the next ten years, we were to walk a **different path**. Duane's recovery became very complicated. His nervous system was messed up; the noise in his head became unbearable and he required a lot of quiet. Within three years, he completely lost his ability to tolerate sound. It was hard to entertain our friends or even have them over for a visit. Family came, but it was hard to keep the little ones quiet. We all felt like we were walking on eggshells. Some of our friends understood, but some didn't. It seemed the least amount of activity or noise made him suffer for days. His outings became very limited and those were only for doctors' visits.

Each day seemed to be a struggle for survival—Duane became a prisoner in his own home. For a man who has always been active, full of life and fun to be with, it is hard to realize that there could be such an extreme loss in such a short time. I accepted his imprisonment for my own. I wanted to be with him, to stand by his side through thick and thin, but there were days on end that I was unable even to read my Bible or pray. I could only repeat the name of Jesus over and over. Sleep was sporadic and I often took my Bible to bed with me just because it was a comfort to touch that beloved Book. I could hold something tangible that communicated God's love, even though I could not understand love that let us suffer so.

Chapter Three

Tammie and Trina

HIS WAYS

John 1:1

"Jesus, if You had been here
Our brother would not have died."
The anguish came from deep within
As Mary and Martha cried.

Jesus felt the agony of their hearts,
The depth of their intense pain.
He knew their brother would live again,
But at the moment He couldn't explain.

There are many things that come in life
That, to us, do not seem fair.
Even though we are children of God,
It **seems like** *He doesn't care.*

At these times our faith is tested;
Like Mary and Martha that day.
God's plan often baffles man,
For He leads us in **His** *way.*

"His ways are not our ways,
They are past finding out."
He only asks that we believe and trust,
Hold fast and refuse to doubt.

The trial will eventually be over;
And the reason will be made plain.
Then we'll lift our hearts in praise to Him,
For our trials become our gain.

Duane D. Logsdon

Chapter 3

Tammie and Trina

June 30, 1995

Summer arrived and the weather was beautiful! Duane and I finished breakfast and the dishes were in the dishwasher. It was a refreshing moment to just look out of the window and admire the flowers. The phone's ring brought me back to reality. "Hello," the voice on the other end was Don. "Mom, it's all over." It seemed that time stood still at that moment. I felt a huge lump in my throat and tears came pouring down my cheeks. "Mom, Tammie passed away about 30 minutes ago. I'm sorry to have to tell you this."

Tammie was our oldest granddaughter, 26 years old, married and the mother of a two-year-old named Brittney Lee. We knew that Tammie had acute lymphoma; we'd known it for two years. She had been in and out of the hospital but we still hoped that the Lord would allow her to get through this.

She was a brave young woman and one who loved the Lord. We shared long telephone calls, letters and visits. Tammie knew she could call us anytime, and we often talked to her several times a day. Duane made cinnamon rolls for her and sent them overnight via UPS from Palm Desert, California (our home for a few months) to the hospital in Seattle, Washington. I shopped for her and sent new pajamas or things I hoped would cheer her up. It didn't seem possible she was with the Lord and her suffering was over. Words cannot describe the loss that we felt.

We grieved her loss for months and we still miss her. Our hearts were broken for Don and Pennie, as they had lost their only other daughter sixteen years before to Cystic Fibrosis. After Trina passed away, Tammie had been their life.

As a family, we were beginning to understand what loss was really all about.

Tammie's story was documented for TV. Many friends in her home community in Nevada prayed for her. The press kept in communication with her and published her progress. Little Brittney was her bone marrow donor. The picture was shown on the front page of the *Reno Gazette Journal* (their local paper). It showed the family boarding a plane from Reno, Nevada, to Seattle, Washington, and the headline in an April 9, 1995 article by Lisa J. Tolda, read, "**Toddler Gives Mom Gift of Life**."[1]

It was at the Fred Hutchinson Medical Center in Seattle where Brittney gave her mother the last chance for life by donating her bone marrow. After Brittney came out of the anesthesia, she grabbed her Grandpa, "Boppie," by the hand. She wanted to see if "Mommie" was well yet. She peeked around the corner of her mother's hospital door and said, "Boo, Mom. Are you well now?" Even now, she still cannot understand why Jesus needed her mother more than she did. However, Brittney and the whole family are seeing how God gives special help to those whose mothers and/or fathers are taken from them. The Psalmist wrote, *"When my father and my mother forsake me (are taken from me), Then the Lord will take care of me"* (Psalm 27:10).

[1] Reno Gazette Journal; April 9, 1995; Article by Lisa J. Tolda.

After work on Fridays, Chad, Tammie's husband, and Don flew from Reno to Seattle to spend the weekends with Tammie. This went on for months. As a family, they rented an apartment close to the hospital so they could take turns being with her. Pennie never wanted to leave her daughter's side. As a family, they gave Tammie love and support during the hardest of times and Brittney was able to be with her Mom every day ... until the last.

The day Tammie went home to be with the Lord, Brittney was able to crawl up into her mother's lap and tell her goodbye, then Don took her down to the hospital rose garden to tell her that Mommie was going to Heaven to be with Jesus. Brittney picked a rose and said, "Can I take Mommie this pretty flower?" Don told her she could. When they arrived back in the room, however, it was empty. Brittney left the rose because she felt Tammie could see it anyway. I'm sure she did. Brittney's comment was, "Mommie doesn't hurt anymore because she's with Jesus."

There is a reason for suffering but we are unable to see its true value here on earth. Nor will we understand why God allows it until we see Him face to face. These are experiences that families go through every day. In the family unit, there should be care and support—especially in such times. But, for one reason or another, not all families have this unity. Often, people find out too late what they could have done to lighten the load of their loved ones. Only later do they realize how much it would have helped just to give a word of encouragement when it was needed most. Failure to do these things can fracture family relationships in such a way that never seem to heal.

Sometimes it takes very little to bridge the gap; just a small act of love that shows we care.

However, the Lord is the source of our deepest and most intimate comfort and purpose ... that is, if we allow Him to be. Slowly, I was learning to reach out to receive that comfort. God does not make mistakes and, for His own reasons, He saw fit to take Tammie at an early age. He decided that her work on earth was finished. Within the plan of God, we all die on time – according to His schedule. I had to trust Him for His reasons.

My mind flashed back to Tammie's sister, Trina, who died seveteen years earlier. Losing a child or a grandchild to an incurable disease is an experience never to be forgotten. Trina had Cystic Fibrosis. She labored to breathe every day of her life. Her food and medication had to be strictly controlled at all times. Nor could Tammie have a normal life knowing that her sister could never do the same things she did or eat the same food she ate. There were many hospitalizations for Trina with pneumonia and in the last few years, she was on oxygen a lot of the time. Physcial therapy on a daily basis was necessary to relieve the congestion in her lungs. Nothing, however, changed the course of the disease.

It was only a few days before Trina passed away that Duane and I went to visit them in Riverside, California. While Duane talked with Pennie and Don downstairs, I stayed upstairs in her room with Trina. Her tape recorder and Bible storybooks were on her bed. We read stories and talked about Heaven. We talked about what a beautiful place it is and that there she (and we, when our turn comes) would see Jesus. She was telling me how she felt about it, when suddenly, she sat up in bed and seemed to talk to someone at the foot of the bed. I heard her say, "But I don't want to leave now; I don't want to leave my Mommie."

I felt like an intruder in a world I could not see. Trina lay back on her pillows and said, "Grandma, someone came for me, but I didn't want to go." The quiet serenity of the moment was disrupted as everyone returned to her room. Pennie told me that Trina had other experiences of someone coming for her.

The next morning, Don and Pennie took Trina to the hospital. She was worsening. The nurse asked the parents to go for a cup of coffee while she readied Trina for the exam. As they turned to leave, Trina said, "Bye, Mommie. Bye, Daddy." Outside the door, Pennie leaned against the wall and sobbed, "Don, she won't be here when we come back. She said her goodbyes."

They could only stay away for a few minutes. Still, when they returned, her room was empty. Trina was freed from her broken body. She was no longer suffering the pain that had plagued her all of her life.

The next few days seemed like a dream. Duane had Trina's graveside service with family and friends. As we stood by the grave, a lady came across the lawn with her arms full of yellow, long-stemmed rose buds. On each rose was a yellow ribbon and the name of each child in Trina's class at school. A tree was later planted at the school in her memory.

We are amazed that Brittney (Trina's niece) who gave her bone marrow to her mother, Tammie, now attends that same school.

"...(God) is the Father of our Lord Jesus Christ, the source of every mercy, and the one who so wonderfully comforts and strengthens us in our hardships and trials. And why does he do this? So that when others are troubled, needing our sympathy and encouragement, we can pass on to them this same help and comfort God has given us."

II Corinthians. 1:3-4 (TLB)

What comfort we find in the Word of God!

"I want you to know what happens to a Christian when he dies so that when it happens, you will not be full of sorrow, as those who have no hope. For since we believe that Jesus died and came back to life again, we can also believe that when Jesus returns, God will bring back with Him all the Christians who have died.... The Lord Himself will come down from heaven with a mighty shout and with the soul-stirring cry of the archangel and the great trumpet call of God. And the believers who are dead will be the first to rise to meet the Lord. Then, we who are still alive and remain on earth will be caught up with them in the clouds to meet the Lord in the air and remain with Him forever. So, comfort each other with this news."

I Thessalonians 4:13-18 (TLB)

We will meet again in triumph! Hallelujah!

Chapter Four

The Shock

STRENGTH AND GRACE

Please grant me strength and grace, Lord.
My desire is to do your will,
To follow Your faithful leading,
Your purpose for life to fulfill.

Now the shadows of trial
Cast darkness across my way.
Your presence I do not feel
Tho' You've promised with me to stay.

Fearful and lonely feelings
Take root within my heart;
They wrestle with truths of God
Which promise You'll never depart.

We're warned to be prepared
For these times are sure to come;
To look to You for strength and grace.
The battles have already been won.

This truth, Oh Lord, my head well knows;
My heart is the battleground.
So Father, my plea to You this day
Is, "Please, keep the enemy bound.

"For I'm no match for him
Without Your sovereign power.
Only in Your strength I shall prevail
For You are my mighty tower."

Duane D. Logsdon

Chapter 4

THE SHOCK

It was mid-afternoon when the fax line rang in our Fullerton home. Since my husband experienced pain in the presence of even the slightest noise, most of our communication with the outside world was done by fax; either my husband or I ran to get the message. Today was no different. However, after reading the first line, we knew this was not going to be a communication of rejoicing.

You may have received the news of a divorce from your child by other means but it still carries the same punch, right at gut level. Maybe the words were:

Dear Mom and Dad,

This is the hardest letter I've ever had to write.

Or maybe you received a call or personal visit, and you hear the words, "I wish I had better news to tell you but...." Maybe you had an adult child land at your front door, announcing, "I need a bed for a few nights because...."

After Duane and I read the fax, we stood looking at each other in stunned disbelief, then anger took hold. The tears flowed and the flood wouldn't stop. I just wanted to smash my fist through the wall. How could this be happening in our family, to our children? I was so angry that my body was shaking and my legs felt like rubber; they wouldn't hold me up. I sat down and wrote a reply, then pushed the start button on the fax machine and watched the letter slowly feed into the machine. It's a wonder the letter did not burn up in the process.

I couldn't believe so much anger could be inside of me. My reaction was a total volatile explosion. After that explosion, I started in on the Lord saying. "Where were You, Lord, when all of this was going on. Why did You allow this to happen?" I demanded.

It took me days to settle down, to try and put this whole matter into perspective. I said hurtful things to others, made improper judgments, and my behavior was anything but kind or Christ-like. In a family unit what hurts one, hurts us all. Regardless of the reasons that bring a couple to the decision of divorce, it changes relationships forever. Many of us have been brought up with the ideal that:

- if we know Christ personally, and
- if we ensure that our children have that same foundation of faith in Christ and
- if they have been raised with Christian values and integrity,

we have the right to expect our little family unit to live "Happily Ever After." We don't anticipate that we might have to experience trials or the disappointment of divorce. Duane and I had especially expected that our children would stay married since they had been raised in a home where their father was a pastor who never even thought about, let alone approved of divorce.

I can see now that this is an unreal expectation ... an ideal. When our ideals were shattered and no longer a reality, we experienced such deep disappointment targeted at the Lord that our fellowship with Him became strained. I felt like my prayers went about as far as the ceiling. I could no longer sense the Lord's presence and it was hard to remember God's love with all the anger and pain I was feeling.

Questions came to mind:

What do parents do when they think they have raised their children in the admonition and nurture of the Lord and things go wrong; when the family unit is shattered by divorce ... or when children choose to part ways with their upbringing and "march to the beat of the world's drummer"?

Did we have the right to believe that being a Christian would exempt our family unit from the pain of life's twists and turns that would cause loss, disunity, disappointment or even separation?

Did we expect you, Lord, only to use our children in positive, loving ways that would glorify You ... and us as parents? Did we have strings attached? Did we expect a bit of glory for a job well done?

Lord, did we really mean it when we dedicated our children and ourselves to you as parents? Did we hold back, have reservations and subconsciously carry unreal expectations?

Did we take into consideration that through the trials, reverses and disappointments of life, You would use these experiences for our growth as a couple, individually and in the lives of our children?

Was our discipline too strong, or not strong enough in raising our children?

Where did we fail them... and You?

All of these questions seemed normal, but my feelings of anger, guilt and disappointment were getting all mixed up with my spiritual life and my identity. This conflict seemed to go on forever. The failure felt like it was my personal failure.

Slowly, we began to realize that we had to:

1. Face This Situation with Reality

We were not superhuman nor super-spiritual, nor could we bury our heads in the sand if we were to have personal victory. Joan Jacobs, in her book, *Feelings*,[1] gives insight into a key issue that both Duane and I had to address:

"When Christians are urged by pastors and teachers to live 'supernaturally,' I'm sure they mean that through God's power in us we should grow to be like Jesus, have His wisdom in decisions and in relationships, and have optimism, courage and discipline in the face of a decaying, sinful world. But many Christians interpret this to mean we must be *superhuman,* and as we try to live at a super level, we're forced to battle the reality of inward problems. We can't take care of the problems because we've put ourselves in the position of having to pretend there aren't any problems. Sometimes we even talk ourselves into thinking

---

[1] *Feelings* by Joan Jacobs; Tyndale Publishers, Inc.; Wheaton IL; Coverdale House Publishers Ltd., Eastbourne, England; p.15.

we have no problems; our ostrich behavior doesn't fool many people."

2. Be Aware of Our Own Emotions

With the shock of this news, I didn't feel like I was growing more like Jesus!! My reactions were:

- Anger (strong feelings of displeasure)
- Bewilderment (being totally confused)
- Bitterness (disagreeable, showing sorrow and pain)
- Depression (low spirits, dejection, feelings of hopelessness).

These feelings were not comfortable nor pretty. A lot of garbage had collected through the years, and most of all, we needed God's love, His insight and His instructions. Duane and I both knew that a difficult growing experience like this could only be borne with tears and determination. We both identified with trying to live at the superhuman level, but we were not going to let go of the Lord until we had His joy and peace.

3. Be Persistent in Identifying Our emotions and Learn to Express Them in a Helathy Way

In *"Feeling Free"*[2], Archibald Hart has written much about our emotions from a Christian point of view:

"The problem of emotions is even more complex for Christians, who must contend with bringing the emotional side of our beings into harmony with our spiritual side.

[2] *Feeling Free*; Archibald D. Hart; Fleming H. Revell Co.; Old Tappan, New Jersey; p. 24.

There are a number of common mistakes that we make as Christians, including the *denial* of feelings, succumbing to emotions in a *defeatist* way, and believing that we are totally *responsible* for everything we feel. A proper attitude toward emotions (along with the recognition that they are God-given and intended to enhance our lives) can free us to experience them in a healthy way."

The battle for accepting this adjustment of divorce was hard work. It seemed like a bad dream and we expected to wake up and find it just that. Reality told us this was not about to happen! This situation was final. The word ADJUST, ADJUST, ADJUST kept haunting our every thought. I didn't *want* to adjust and hanging onto the anger seemed to be more comfortable than changing my mind.

After much turmoil and many sleepless nights, this problem seemed to permeate every part of my body. Duane and I often talked way into the morning hours. It was comforting to retreat to the four walls of our home; visits with close friends became an intrusion into this private world of pain. There were days on end when my daily work was done without planning or thought. My favorite place was the big chair in our family room looking out of the window at the pool, listening to the birds and watching the flowers grow.

Anger finally gave place to simply wanting to be alone with the Lord and to feel the comfort of His Word—nothing else mattered.

Only the Lord knows the unique experiences that will draw us unto Himself, whether it is for salvation or for a closer walk with Him. When we meet Him face to face, we will understand why He has allowed each of our experiences. He doesn't want us to miss out on any experience of spiritual growth that has eternal value. We will see for ourselves how in our trials, through His grace and strength, He revealed Himself in love for our good and His glory. It takes an experience like a divorce in the family for ALL of us to realize that we are not as godly as we thought we were and that we are not exempt from the trials of life. This was definitely an experience of shattered ideals!

We desperately needed people around us who would be our support, people that would have the patience just to love us in our arduous growing state. We desired to work with a godly counselor to help us through the maze. Many times, we (Christians) are the last to look into the Word to see *who* we "are" and *what* we "are" when the chips are down. However, there comes a time when we must come to grips with our pain, see our reactions to that pain and do something about it or we will stunt our own spiritual growth with self-pity, anger and defeat. Besides that, a lot of people around us will suffer, too.

God has only good in mind for us; He is changing us into the image of His dear Son who knew a great deal about suffering. In these hard times of change and adjustment, we continue to develop a love relationship with Him, we are to trust His promises in all of our circumstances and believe that He has a plan and purpose for each one of us. This faith includes the lives of our children who are struggling to survive as well. He has told us in the Scriptures:

"For I know the plans I have for you, says the Lord. They are plans for good and not for evil, to give you a future and a hope."

Jeremiah 29:11 (TLB)

"We live within the shadow of the Almighty, sheltered by the God who is above all gods. This I declare, that he alone is my refuge, my place of safety; he is my God, I am trusting him."

Psalm 91: 1-2 (TLB)

Chapter Five

Depression-Big Time!

IN NEED

Lord, I'm feeling down today;
I really don't know why.
I've searched my heart. That hasn't helped:
I feel I'd like to cry.

It would be nice to sense Your presence,
Feel Your gentle touch.
Father, I'm not being selfish,
I really need You very much

You said that we'd have times like this
And loneliness and pain,
But promised that You'd walk with us,
Our fears are all in vain.

Help me to accept these things -
Not worry how I feel;
Believe Your Word, give You my heart,
Your presence to reveal.

Duane D. Logsdon

Chapter 5

DEPRESSION—BIG TIME!

Divorce shatters a family like an egg falling on the kitchen floor, and each family member is left to struggle and to try to accept it, personally coping with it the best way possible. Emotional pieces of my heart were scattered all over the place. It felt like another death in the family; one goes through the same process of loss in bereavement. There are feelings of failure as a parent and failure as a person. Since it was our adult child who faced divorce, our whole family unit seemed to blow up as if a bomb had been detonated!

Little did Duane and I know that in the months to come, we would walk this way **three more times**. By the time the fourth divorce was announced, Duane and I were numb and void of feeling. We started out with anger at the news of the first divorce; now we felt destroyed, void of life and through with living.

On top of Duane's physical problems and the divorces, loneliness was added to our life of isolation. We shared the devastating emotions and pain that our sons were going through. The loss of each daughter-in-law seemed unbearable. Each of the girls has a special place in our hearts. We felt robbed of the daughters that God gave us through the marriages of our sons. These dear women were part of our family for at least seventeen years, and as long as twenty-six years. They bore our grandchildren and we still want a relationship with them even though it must, of necessity, be different. One of the girls became a part of our family when she was in the third grade. On family vacations, our niece used to invite her little friend because all the other cousins were boys, and that little girl later married into the family. We still love them and pray for them. Duane and I tried hard not to interfere in our children's home life or marriages. We never even visited them without calling first.

In those days, we felt that even God had forgotten us. The following turn of events made us wonder even more.

It was a bright sunshiny day and it was nice to have Duane in the car beside me. We were on our way to see Dr. Royce Hutain, our family doctor, for Duane's regular routine physical exam. You know how these things go; you're glad to get this yearly thing over and you really expect everything to be normal since you don't go with any specific complaint. While Duane was busy with the doctor, the office was quiet so, getting comfortable in the chair, I took a book out of my purse, one that I could get lost in and be absorbed for an hour or so. A few days after Duane's physical, we were told, however, that all was not fine. There were some abnormalities.

Next, we were sent to the office of Dr. Paul Ovando, a surgeon and specialist of thoracic and cardiovascular problems. It was there we learned that Duane had a lung tumor. Surgery for the biopsy was scheduled in three weeks.

This time, three of the boys were with us, along with Renee and Pennie. David was in South Carolina completing his doctorate. He kept in constant contact through both surgeries and Duane's recovery time. This first surgery was a 5-1/2 hour operation and very hard on Duane. He was allergic to most pain medication. After waiting for the lab reports, we were told the tests were positive and the tumor in the upper right lung, was malignant. The next surgery was scheduled ten days later when the upper lobe of the right lung was to be removed.

This was another 5-1/2 hour surgery. For the next five days, we all took turns being with Duane night and day. When we brought him home, our next course of treatments would start in a few weeks—25 treatments of radiation. His recovery was slow but we were thankful that he was still with us.

These surgeries complicated the ear problems and Duane's confinement became more defined. I seldom left the house and then only to run essential errands and to buy groceries. There was a lot of time to think, pray and read my Bible. I went through the motions, but (unrecognized by me) I was in depression. I read God's words but could not apply the comforts that were available to me. I dropped out of church and it was months before I started attending again.

I felt totally alone in a crowd; I felt "different" and distant even with my friends. I didn't belong any place, including my church, nor did I want to go anywhere. Besides that, we were wearing our friends out sending cards to cheer us, letters to encourage us and hours of prayer on our behalf. Depression hit me big time! It was more comfortable to isolate myself, to keep the doors locked and the curtains closed. Now we were dealing with three severe problems—multiple health problems, a family that was disintegrating and my depression.

At the same time, the boys seemed to be saying to me, "What's your problem, Mom? The divorces are our problem, NOT YOURS. We feel the same loss; snap out of it." Our boys were kind enough, however, that though they may have thought this, they never said it. They were all hurting and tried to be truthful with us. At the same time, they were stressed over the hurt that it caused us. They visited us when they could; they wrote or called us; some called several times a week. They were working hard to manage their own survival. Our communication never stopped and they remained concerned about the health and stress problems that Duane and I faced daily. Yet, it seemed everywhere I turned, I heard the words, "Snap out of it, SNAP OUT OF IT, SNAP OUT OF IT!" But I just couldn't.

When I did go to church I came home discouraged, vowing not to go back. Being there, yet alone in a crowd was too painful. Somehow the book, How To Help A Heartbroken Friend by David Biebel, found its way into our mailbox. As I read it, the following lines seemed to magnify my feelings. These comments were taken out of a story about a lady being alone in a crowd at church:

> *Our hypothetical church service has gotten beyond the announcements, hymns, special music, and the offering, but you still haven't zeroed in on anybody who seems to listen to what the guest speaker is saying.*
>
> *"Listen, grump," he says. "You know what your problem is? It's your attitude! Life has its problems. We all know that. Nobody said it would be easy, but*

why all the doom and gloom? Everybody falls into a pit once in a while, but you don't have to wallow in it, throwing a pity party nobody wants to attend. We're not pigs ... we're eagles, who on wings of faith can rise above anything and everything the devil throws our way.

"Did you wake up this morning with a chip on your shoulder? Then get back into the bed and get out on the other side! Happiness is a choice, after all. If you're depressed, it's because you want to be depressed. If you can't see the bright side of life, it's because you don't want to. There's no other logical - or spiritual reason.

"You've got to take off those melancholy spectacles and look at life with positive eyes of faith! God gave you two eyes for a reason. Some people gaze at their problem with both eyes and never look at God. Some gaze at the problem with one eye and glance at God with the other. Some glance at the problem with one eye and gaze at God with the other. But the only way to live the victorious life is to gaze at God with both eyes, and never give those problems the slightest glance."[1]

At one point, I even went forward after a service to ask for prayer. After waiting for about fifteen minutes for a counselor, a young lady came running breathlessly from the

---

[1] *How To Help a Heartbroken Friend,* David Biebel; Published by Fleming H. Revell, a division of Baker Books; P.O. Box 6287, Grand Rapids, MI 49516-6287; pg. 5.

parking lot of the church to pray with me. Her prayer was, "Please, Lord, help this lady find some friends in our church." Needless to say, I went home rather empty. As Dr. Biebel stated, sometimes we feel like "...an alien, disconnected from everybody."[2]

"I would have lost heart unless I had believed I would see the goodness of the Lord in the land of the living.

Wait on the Lord; be of good courage, and He shall strengthen your heart; Wait I say, on the Lord"

(Psalm 27: 13-14).

There was only one place to go and that was to the Lord, and there to WAIT ON HIM.

What did I expect of my church, friends and family? Why did I even go forward for prayer? I really love my church. Why did I feel so let down, angry and at a loss for words? Was I so untouchable in my emotions or Christian maturity that I had turned into a complaining, demanding, critical child of God?

It seemed others saw my pain as fixable:

- Do something for others. It will help an ugly attitude and relieve your feelings of self-pity.
- Maybe you need professional help or a more mature attitude about trusting the Lord.
- Maybe it is something in your past. You may need to explore the why of God's anger.

---

[2] Op.cit., pg.6.

Larry Crabb wrote the answers so beautifully in his book, *The Safest Place on Earth*:

"I longed for my friends to enter my world, to be intrigued with what God was doing in (my life), to ask questions, to honor (my) place in the journey and do it all with no agenda. I did not want them to offer what our therapy-mad culture thinks is helpful: to look for pathology that can be fixed.

"Yet you can hear your own heart crying, 'It's You, Lord, that I want.' In the Lord, I take my refuge. I don't want to run to a mountain of relief. Lead me into the presence of God. Everything else is secondary!"[3]

Mrs. Charles Cowman wrote in *"Streams in the Desert":*

"How the soul sinks, the heart grows sick, and faith staggers under the keen trials and testings which come into our lives of special bereavement and sufferings.... When we are tempted to faint under affliction, God's message to us is not, *"Be strong and of good courage"* for He knows our strength and courage have fled away. His message is that sweet word, *"Be still, and know that I am God."*[4]

---

[3] Larry Crabb: *The Safest Place on Earth,* 1999; Word Publishing, Nashville, a Thomas Nelson Company, pg. 15,19.

[4] Mrs. Charles Cowman; *Streams in the Desert;* Cowman Publications, Inc.; Publishers: Zondervan Publishing House, Grand Rapids, Michigan 49506; p.142.

Chapter Six

Adjustments

WAITING

There are some things that come in life
That we can't understand.
God does not reveal His plan to us
We must accept it from His hand.

It often makes no sense to us,
Our minds can't comprehend.
For He is God who controls all things.
He says this trial will end.

The only way to accept this truth
Is through a gift called faith
Enabling us to trust His Word
And then just rest and wait.

His promises will come to pass
In His time, and in His way.
Until they do, we must hold fast.
His Word we must obey.

At last, this test will all be done
His full plan will unfold.
Our hearts will leap in joy sublime.
It will be as we were told.

Duane Logsdon

Chapter 6

ADJUSTMENTS

The aroma of coffee filled the kitchen and the clock on the microwave said 4:30 A.M. For me, the night had been sleepless. I kept praying:

> Lord, you have promised that You will "never leave us or forsake us."[1] Yet ... right now I feel like You are just some place *out there.* When I see other couples our age enjoying new-found freedom which they share, I covet what they have and I'm sorry. You have allowed so many reverses in our lives that we have lost our joy and our purpose for living. If you are not going to change our circumstances, PLEASE change our attitudes and our hearts. Lord, I won't let You go… we need Your joy, Your strength and Your victory regardless of our circumstances."

With this prayer on my lips and a cup of coffee in my hand, I walked toward the family room to sit in the old green chair, once again to spend time with my Lord and in His Word.

There were times between reading and praying that my mind flashed back to all the adjustments we had made.

---

[1] *Let your conduct be without covetousness; be content with such things as you have. For He Himself has said, "I will never leave you nor forsake you"* (Hebrews 13:5-6 NIV).

Because of Duane's physical limitations requiring us to regulate sound at a comfortable level for him, our home environment had changed.

- Music no longer filled the rooms of our home.
- Meals were taken in the dining room because the kitchen refrigerator was too noisy. (Can you imagine two people eating three meals a day at a table for eight? Only we didn't have a butler!)
- Visits by family and friends were limited. (The visits often created so much distress that Duane had to spend several days in bed recuperating.)
- There was no more going out to eat, going to church as a couple, not even any riding in the car just for the joy of riding.
- Food was selected and prepared specially—nothing too loud and crunchy.
- The ringer on the telephone had special adjustments.
- I used a secluded room to watch TV so Duane could remain in the family room.
- We became aware of crinkling paper, running water, lawn mowers, blowers, silverware hitting against dishes, the microwave, the computer and the vacuum cleaner. The patio was also off limits because of street noise. THERE WAS NO END to the adjustments!

Under ordinary circumstances, we don't think of these things as being irritating. We go about our day and are oblivious to these sounds, but Duane and I could not ignore them. It seemed our lives consisted of dealing with physical disability and loss.

Dan Malcore, Founder/Editor of the Hyperacusis Network, has so ably described what Hyperacusis, Recruitment and Tinnitus is all about (Duane had all three of these conditions). This will give you some idea of what these people suffer:

> To Individuals and Families experiencing the trauma of Hyperacusis and Recruitment:
>
> Many parents and adults have asked me—*What is it like to have extremely sensitive hearing?* Those with hyperacusis, recruitment and/or severe tinnitus try to communicate their difficulties to family and friends. They find themselves misunderstood, isolated and lonely. Allow me a few minutes to speak on behalf of those of us who have "delicate" ears. Although all of us have different sensitivities (tolerances), many of the things mentioned here will most assuredly apply to you or your loved one. Hopefully in some small way this will help you understand what we are going through. When the words "us" or "we" are used, I am referring to everyone in the world that communicates regularly to a network of individuals who have collapsed tolerance to sound. This includes individuals with hyperacusis, recruitment, vestibular disorders and even autistic children. God made us all unique. Not one of us has the same degree of difficulty with sound. Much of what is said here will address the main problem areas. Many

with hyperacusis or recruitment also suffer with varying degrees of tinnitus (ringing in the ears and head noises). All of these conditions can be disabling depending on their severity. For many of us, our problem is three-fold. Our collapsed tolerance to sound means we have a difficult time listening to sounds which exceed 50 decibels (the sound of someone talking). Secondly, our dynamic range is very narrow whereby it is difficult for us to handle quick shifts in noise intensity. Thirdly, tinnitus (ringing in the ears or head noises) disrupts even our quiet time. Some of us have far more problems than we are about to address here and some have far less. Some of us have gotten better over time and some have gotten worse. Time is clearly the best healer after a noise injury. No one knows the answer to solving our condition but some clues are beginning to surface.[2]

While hyperacusis is an abnormal sensitivity to sound,[3] recruitment is a measurable hearing loss, which can be clearly documented on an audiometer. For people with recruitment, some frequencies or sounds cannot be heard (birds chirping), while others suddenly become too

---

2 *Hyperacusis Network Supplement;* Dan Malcore, Founder/Editor; 120 Traders Point Lane, Green Bay, Wisconsin 54302.

3 *Taber's Cyclopedic Medical Dictionary;* F. A. Davis Co., 1915 Arch St., Philadelphia, Pa., 19103; pg. H-68.

loud.[4] Tinnitus is a subjective ringing, tingling, buzzing or other sounds in the ear.[5]

While Duane was trying to cope with his world, I was also beginning to feel very dysfunctional in the world outside our four walls. This caused feelings of useless-ness and being unloved by everyone, including our family. Everyone seemed so busy and going on with their own lives at a very fast pace, while our life was standing still. This caused me frustration and discouragement.

When the weeks turned into years, we realized that people forget and we lost contact with many who were once a vital part of our life. Gradually, we were being cut off. This was one reason the divorces of all four of the boys seemed so intense. We felt isolated—without our friends, we were losing our ability to cope with life as our family was torn apart by separation.

At one time, we felt assured that God would heal Duane and we would be able to go on living as before. However as time wore on, that did *not* seem to be in the Lord's plan; it did not materialize. Since this was the case, for us to survive with any measure of sanity, God had to change us from the inside. We were desperate enough to be willing!

---

[4] *Hyperacusis Network Supplement;* Dan Malcore, Founder/Editor; 120 Traders Point Lane, Green Bay, Wisconsin 54302; pg. 2.

[5] *Taber's Cyclopedic Medical Dictionary;* F. A. Davis Co.; 1915 Arch St., Philadelphia, Pa. 19103; pg. T-43

Little did we understand that God was molding us more nearly into the image of His dear Son than we had ever been before. The refiner's fire turns dull rock into molten liquid so the impurities can rise to the top and be skimmed off, leaving pure gold. We were in the fire all right. And the impurities were definitely rising to the top.

We struggled feverishly to remember that *He* is the refiner and *He* will remove the impurities until Christ can be seen shining through our hearts and lives. Just then, however, we were more aware of the heat of suffering around us and the inadequacy of our faith than we were of God's hand on our lives. He seemed remote *although He was actually close at hand,* working to honor and glorify His Son in us.

Chapter Seven

The Search

I BELIEVE

I believe the things I know
And with others I have shared.
I want to say, "It'll be okay,
From this pain I'll soon be spared."

I want to shout, "Deliverance has come
All will soon be well."
I have no way of knowing when;
For only time will tell.

Some of the trials God allows to come
Are hard and filled with pain.
He only lets us experience these things,
To test our faith in the strain.

I must be very patient
For with me He's walking through
This difficult time of testing and tears.
Before it began, He knew.

He knew it would be a test of faith
Designed to try my soul,
And when it has passed, I'll feel at last
That again I am made whole.

Then I will say, as I do today,
"I believe the things that I know,
God's Word is true, He has seen me through
Every trial, wherever I'm called to go."

Duane D. Logsdon

Chapter 7

THE SEARCH

The office was very quiet; and so were all the people inside. Some read magazines, a few stared at the floor or ceiling, others were busy writing notes. Upon entering the door, I noticed there was a plaque at eye level that said, "Henslin and Associates." After a few minutes, an inner office door opened and a very handsome couple walked ahead of their counselor exchanging a "thank you" as they parted. I felt a little on edge being here, not knowing what to expect, or for that matter, why specifically I was even here. All I knew was that I needed help! There was a hole in my heart that was as big as all outdoors. Friends tried to help me, but their efforts proved fruitless. The wonderful messages at church were not helping, and the prayer room episode seemed to make things worse. Besides that, the Lord had not changed my attitude *or* my circumstances. Things just kept getting darker. I was completely miserable.

There was some comfort in isolating myself inside the four walls of our home. There was comfort in reading the Scriptures because it gave daily strength. When I read about David and Job in the Old Testament, it was comforting because they both shared their emotions and grief with truthfulness and honesty. They shared their family tragedies and turmoil. They revealed their broken health problems and disappointment with God, but they never gave up on God. Our time alone with the Lord and reading the Scriptures was our daily source of strength and our only means of survival! However, for some reason, neither

Duane nor I were able to apply what we heard or read. There was definitely something missing. We talked and it was decided that I would seek counseling with Dr. Earl Henslin in nearby Brea, California. (Later Duane followed with personal counseling as well.) Earl is not just *any* counselor. He is also a godly man who loves the Lord; in fact, his entire staff are Christians. He is well known for his publications, books, and seminars (at home and abroad). He has a reputation for helping many hurting people. He is also an educator, teaching periodically at the Rosemead School of Psychology in La Mirada, California. Duane and I both felt confident about our decision and my appointment was scheduled.

Divorce was the topic that Dr. Earl and I discussed. Since divorce had never pushed its ugly head into our thinking, Duane and I still believed that going through the court system to undo vows that two people had made before God, was not right. When we were married, we promised to love, honor and cherish each other regardless of our circumstances. I'm not saying that we never had a disagreement, because in our 48 years of marriage we had plenty of them. When we were first married, Duane hung up his bath towel in an irritating manner and, besides that, he squeezed the toothpaste tube the wrong way. However, our differences never touched the foundation of our marriage. I think the closest time we ever came to this was when I swapped his prize-hunting dog for a bag of walnuts. That was a very destructive dog! We both made mistakes, but we grew in our marriage relationship together. It takes practice, work and sacrifice to make a marriage work, but we loved each other enough to listen and be honest, truthful and faithful in our commitment to one another.

The vows we said before God, family and friends were to be until "death do us part."[1] The ideal for our family was that our sons and their wives should feel the same way. However, we could not force our value system on them or keep harassing them with it. They were adults—we could only pray and be available to stand by them. Besides that, some of our boys had no choice in the decision about their divorces—but at the same time, we knew it took two to make it happen.

As Duane and I worked through our own needs, it became evident that we could not be of help to anyone, including ourselves, until we had the desire and strength to change the damaging emotions that were tearing us apart. We knew that apart from the Lord, in-depth counseling and the patience of our family and friends, we could not do it. We felt as though our value system as Christian parents was being recycled! We questioned our own shortcomings and wondered what we had done to these children to have caused them so much unhappiness in their own lives and homes. In the book, *Real Family Values* by Robert Lewis, we were impressed by what he said about the responsibilities of a parent:

> We believe that the Christian parent (I Timothy 5:8; Ephesians 6:4; Deuteronomy 6:6-7; I Timothy 4:16 Proverbs 22:6) is responsible to:

---

[1] Mark 10: 6-9 (NKJV), "*But from the beginning of creation, God made them male and female. For this reason a man shall leave his father and mother and be joined to his wife and the two shall be one flesh; so then they are no longer two, but one flesh. Therefore what God has joined together, let no man separate.*"

- Provide for the children's physical needs.[2]
- Provide a safe haven of unconditional love and affection.[3]
- Provide guidance, boundaries, affirmation, and correction.[4]
- Teach knowledge of God and character values by model and instruction.[5]
- Understand the children and seek to help them develop their spiritual gifts and personalities.[6]/[7]

---

[2] I Timothy 5:8 (NAS), "*But if any one does not provide for his own, and especially for those of his household, he has denied the faith, and is worse that an unbeliever.*"

[3] Ephesians 6:4 (NAS), "*And fathers, do not provoke your children to anger; but bring them up in the discipline and instruction of the Lord.*"

[4] Deuteronomy 6:6,7 (NAS), "*And these words, which I am commanding you today, shall be on your heart; and you shall teach them diligently to your sons and shall talk of them when you sit in your houses and you walk by the way and when you lie down and when you rise up.*"

[5] I Timothy 4:16 (NAS), "*Pay close attention to yourself and to your teaching; persevere in these things; for as you do this you will insure salvation both for yourself and for those who hear you.*"

[6] Proverbs 22:6, "*Train up a child in the way that he should go, even when he is old he will not depart from it.*"

[7] *Real Family Values*, Robert Lewis; © 1995 Vision House Publishing, Inc.; Greshem, Oregon 97030, pg. 96.

These values we tried to impart to our children in the raising of our family. That doesn't mean we were perfect parents, but we did the best we could with what we had to do with.

The longer this counseling session lasted, the more I realized that Duane and I had some reconciliation work to do with our family. There were apologies that needed to be made and forgiveness to be asked for. Being pious, judgmental or holding grudges was not the answer.

Chuck Swindoll wrote in his book, *Come Before Winter*, these words:

> "We must be discerning, alert, even mindful that human depravity must be held in check, and on occasion it must be exposed. But the way we do it, the spirit in which we handle our conflict, the attitudes we exhibit while working through the process of reconciliation is crucial ... that is where our Christianity is often hung out to dry."[8]

Dr. Earl emphasized, "More often than not, we are blind to our own shortcomings or how we have hurt others. Then when the Lord shows us our true attitudes and behaviors, we are appalled at the depth of our own deceit. Divorce in a family brings out the worst in us." We did have bitter feelings about why our children did not see the danger signals in their marriages and get help before it was too late. We were bitter with the parties that would not

---

[8] *Come Before Winter*; © 1985 by Charles Swindoll, Inc.; Published by Multnomah Press; Portland, OR 92266, pg, 66.

change their ways for the sake of their marriage or the welfare of their children. It seemed there was so much selfishness and no flexibility. We were bitter about what these divorces were doing to our grandchildren and some of the actions of "mate-hate"[9] that was going on. It all seemed so unnecessary.

Our own healing would start when we focused on cleaning up our own lives and attitudes! Dr. Earl Henslin said, "We can't sweep negative emotions under the rug. They will come out in other ways. Many times we pay the price with our own physical or mental health."

Frankly, Duane and I were sick of being "walking wounded."[10] We did not want to be "bitter old people" or "finger pointers," blaming others for the stalemate in which we found ourselves.

The counseling session ended with these choices:

- Would Duane and I be brave enough to want to see ourselves as the Lord sees us?
- Would we be forthright enough to ask others for forgiveness (words harshly said, anger, bitterness, judgmental attitude)?
- Would we be willing to surrender our hurts to the Lord and let Him change us? (This cannot be done without His power nor without our consent and willingness to let Him change us).

---

[9] "Mate-hate" is a phrase borrowed from Dr. Clyde Narramore; *Parents At Their Best*; © 1985; Thomas Nelson Publishers, Inc., Nashville, Tennessee, pg. 52.
[10] Rev. Bob Kraning; borrowed "walking wounded" phrase; Chapel Service sermon; First Evangelical Free Church, Brea, CA 92635.

The choice was ours. Life had dealt us a hard blow, but everyone has experiences that disappoint, hurt, and give others a look at our humanity. It's called "life." Someday, he promised, this experience would become a positive experience because we would grow individually and the Lord would not leave us. God has promised never to leave us. Just because we do not sense His presence does not mean that He is not there!

> "*...for He Himself has said, I will never desert you, nor will I forsake you*" Hebrews 13:5 (NAS).

Chapter Eight

I'll Walk With You

I'll Walk With You

"Be still and know that I am God."
His Word tells us so to do.
My heart cries out, "Oh Lord, I can't,
Somehow I can't even find You;

Daily battles I must fight,
And all I know is pain."
His still small voice comes back to me,
"My child, it's not in vain.

"Life is filled with times of test,
It's the way for you to grow.
You're being prepared for Heaven's scene,
Where joy and peace you'll know.

So, as you go through these things
I'll walk with you and give,
The grace and strength required
And the peace with which to live.

Just let Me bear your load;
Please take Me by the hand.
We'll walk together the paths of life
To your home in Heaven's land.

So take heart, my child, and heed my word
And learn to trust and be still;
New strength you'll find for the journey of life,
As you look forward to Heaven's thrill.

Duane D. Logsdon

Chapter Eight

I'LL WALK WITH YOU

Our school of hard knocks was not yet over!!! Again, we were to hear (with our souls, not with our ears) the words, ADJUST, ADJUST, ADJUST!

Duane had not been feeling well for several weeks, but we passed it off as circumstantial. We continued our counseling with Dr. Earl at our home. Being confined to the four walls of our home for eight and a half years and suffering pain even at the sound of a human voice, had a way of working overtime on the nervous system.

We scheduled an appointment with our primary care doctor for the routine check-up of a physical. Duane had been complaining about a pain under his arm but there was no outward indication of anything unusual. We went home to await the results of the tests.

A week passed when our concerns became fears. Something was wrong ... had the cancer metastasized? Fourteen months had passed since Duane had the upper lobe of his right lung removed because of cancer. Our struggle and pain with the divorce situations in our family took on a lesser degree of concern. However, the ache was still there mixed with anticipation of even greater loss.

The hands on the clock seemed to stand still. I couldn't call Dr. Ovando until 10:00 A.M. so Duane and I talked about the swelling under his arm and what it might mean. The scariest thoughts were not mentioned as we tried not to alarm one another unnecessarily.

Once again our ten-minute drive to the doctor's office seemed to take an eternity since we both dreaded this visit. This was a re-run of our nightmare fourteen months earlier. Dr. Ovando, Duane's surgeon, had been called at the hospital, his staff telling us to be in his office at 10:30 A.M.

"Duane, what have you got going here?" the doctor said with a very winsome smile. As Duane talked to him, I watched that smile fade as he examined the swelling and asked Duane to lie down on the examining table. When he asked Chris, his assistant, to hand him the ruler and a marking pen, I noticed that smile change to deep concern. Having been trained as a medical assistant, I knew he was marking off the outline of a tumor. I felt sick to my stomach and wanted to burst into tears, "NO GOD, THIS CAN'T BE HAPPENING AGAIN ... NOT WITH EVERYTHING ELSE GOING ON." We were both in shock as plans were made for "out-patient" surgery on Monday morning. We left the doctor's office and went immediately to St. Jude Hospital to have the pre-surgical lab work done.

Again we talked with our sons; Don would fly down from Nevada for the weekend and be with us for several days. There is nothing like your family to give you support at a time like this.

I looked at the clock. At 1:30 P.M., the waiting room was almost empty. Most of the surgeries had been completed and folks had taken their love ones home. The nurse called Duane and took him down the hall to start his I.V. and to finish his preparation for the surgery. Don and I were amazed at the way Duane was handling this whole matter. Even with the odds stacked against him, his countenance was that of peace. He had settled the coming verdict, whatever it was, with the Lord. He was not looking forward to another surgery, but he was at peace. He asked us to have prayer together before we left for the hospital.

It seemed so strange that this could be happening again… but it was. There was no turning back, no bargaining with God. Our faith said that the Lord would be with us this time, too. He promised this in His Word:

"Do not fear, for I am with you.
Do not be anxiously looking about you, for I am your God.
I will strengthen you; surely I will help you,
Surely I will uphold you with My righteous right hand."
Isaiah 41:10

It was later that our familiar nurse returned and invited Don and me to have a few words with Duane before the doctor came. Their care for his comfort had all been arranged. In consideration of his hearing problem, he was again put into a glassed-in, isolation area to shield him from any harsh sounds. Chris had arranged all of this along with signs to the hospital staff for them to be as quiet as possible. Since this was a worry for both of us, we appreciated the policy of St. Jude for "special care" to those who needed it.

Our time together was short, then we watched the staff take him through another set of swinging doors. We gazed after him as he smiled and kidded with the doctor about making a neat incision, just like the rest of them. We heard him say, "Man, you've already got me looking like I've met Zorro." Don and I returned to the waiting room… to wait some more.

In a very short period of time, we noticed Dr. Ovando and Chris coming down the hall. In that brief moment I studied their faces, their eyes, and their walk. Was there anything that would give away their mission? I looked for a smile, but there was none.

"I'm sorry," said the doctor. "I don't have very good news. I wish I had something to comfort your heart at this time, but I don't." Dr. Ovando revealed that the tumor was so invasive and large that they had just closed the incision. He showed us pictures that were taken; there was nothing more he could say or do. I'm sure this is never easy for any doctor, an assistant or a nurse. I wondered how many times that day Dr. Ovando had told a family this same kind of devastating news. We waited for Duane to feel better and for the time when he would be released so we could take him home. I did a lot of crying behind some doors when we got home.

In a few days, we returned to the hospital radiology department to see Dr. Patricia Tretter. Duane was again x-rayed, measured and tattooed in preparation for another 25 treatments of radiation, plus five booster treatments. This would make 55 radiation treatments in less than 16 months.

Dr. Tretter became the "other woman" in Duane's life. She offered support and love to both of us along with expertise and knowledge in her field. She is a person who understands people who are sick and hurting. She was always up and was able to raise our spirits constantly while we shared hugs and tears. She cared!

It was several weeks after this that we got the news that the fourth divorce in our family was final. This did not come as a surprise as we were prepared; we had known for some weeks that it was inevitable. This did not mean we stopped praying, loving and caring for our son and "daughter-in-love," but at this time, we were consumed with life and death matters. We were overwhelmed in trying to work through all of the negatives.

These experiences, being our outward circumstances, presented a very important observation that we had to address in the light of God's Word. If there was ever a time that we were to learn the **difference between happiness and joy,** it was now. We had been told that "happiness" depends on what "happens" to us, while our joy is found in Jesus regardless of life's circumstances. We were soon to have a better understanding of this truth.

It was still dark outside when my day began. Making my way to the kitchen to make a cup of coffee, my mind kept turning to the subject of happiness and joy. My heart was heavy when I took the cup of steaming coffee in my hand and headed for the old green chair and my Bible. It seemed to me that happiness and joy were just an illusion. I felt discouraged, afraid, unsettled and very tired. It was easy to dwell on our losses by continually looking back on happier times with each other and as a family. It seemed unavoidable to fall into this joyless, depressive state of grief. I seemed to wander through the rest of the day with this same spirit—that is, until the mail came.

The card of encouragement was mixed in with all of the junk mail which was readily tossed aside. I could hardly wait to get the envelope open as it was from a friend we had not seen in forty years. Our husbands had been in college together and we had been neighbors for four years. Tucked inside the card was a tract.

After reading Barbara's words of comfort, I stared at the tract for a long time before reading it. It was because of Barbara Grandstaff's walk of faith through unbelievable circumstances that I took time out to read it. How could Barbara live through the tragic automobile accident and recovery of her daughter, a hunting accident that took the life of her husband only to live through almost the same accident years later with the death of her son? Barbara wrote encouraging words to us about her joy in the Lord—even when her heart was breaking—and how the Lord had been faithful to her through those difficult years. We needed to hear this.

The scripture verse inside the tract was:

"*...do not be grieved*
for the joy of the Lord is your strength."

Nehemiah 8: 10 b

Somehow, we were not applying this truth to our lives.

My Bible reading for that day was Isaiah 43:18-19. It caught my attention when I first read it. Now, with a compelling desire, I wanted to re-read it. So ... back to the Bible and the "old green chair." Then, I had to share this with Duane immediately. Here was something the Lord was telling us.

"*Do not call to mind the former things*
or ponder things of the past.
Behold I will do something new;
now it will spring forth;
will you be aware of it?

I will even make a roadway in the wilderness,
rivers in the desert."

To us, this was not some mystic experience. We felt the Lord was giving us a key promise. He would do something new; now would we be aware of it? A quote from the tract by Terry A. Anderson says it so simply:

"Sorrow and pain may be present at various times in our lives, but joy has the capacity to cover the suffering with mental and emotional strength."[1]

He emphasizes that our joy in the Lord causes us to have CONFIDENCE and TRUST in Him (the Lord) and in His Word when we cannot see the purpose for our circumstances. Thus, *happiness* is a result of events and circumstances. *Joy* is found only in the Lord.

I folded the card and returned it to the envelope with a thankful heart that Barbara had taken the time to write and share her testimony of victory, and that she loved us enough to be concerned about our joy in the Lord. Again Duane and I talked about what was ahead for us. We both desired that others might see the miracle of joy in the Lord at work in our lives as well. We would live each day as if it were our last, with confidence in the Lord, and we would trust in His powerful Word. We looked at each other and vowed, by God's grace to HANG IN THERE UNTIL GOD CALLED US HOME. We would completely leave IN HIS CARE those things we couldn't change.

---

[1] *Joy Out Of Sorrow and Pain*; © 1988 by Alive, Inc.; published by New Life Publishing; P. 0. Box 1018, Blanco, TX 78606; pg. I I.

Most of the day was spent with these thoughts in mind.

Later in the evening a big blessing was in store.

The doorbell broke the silence of our home and our personal thoughts. Opening the door, we found Dr. Earl Henslin, our friend and counselor. His arms were loaded with flowers, a beautifully-wrapped gift, an ice cream cake from 31-Flavors and flying over his head was a big balloon that said, "Happy anniversary."

With a big smile on his face, he said, "Hope I'm not too late to help you celebrate. You both mentioned that though you were married in August, you had been seeing each other before that … so, I'm here to celebrate the fiftieth anniversary of your dating!"

We were stunned at this man's love and sensitivity. We had been married almost fifty years, but we had both given up the thought of celebrating this special milestone.

Of course, there were tears, hugs and prayers of thanksgiving as we shared this very intimate moment with our friend. When it came time to open the gift, we found a clock and on the face of it were two angels. One lifted its head to give the other a kiss. How fitting!

"Yes, Lord, You are doing something new. And yes, Lord, we are aware of it. We also hold Your promise dear to us that You will make 'a roadway in the wilderness and rivers in the desert.'"

Chapter Nine

"Our World" Torn Apart

HEAVEN BOUND

Heaven wouldn't be the same
If all life's path were smooth;
For it's the struggle and the pain
That God will often use.

It's the valleys and the tears
That I face while traveling home
That creates in me a longing
To join that heavenly throng.

There I'll know no days of sadness
Filled with pain and tears.
There I'll know just joy and gladness
No more sorrow, no more fears.

For the Lord I love and serve
Will be there to welcome me.
He'll reach out and take my hand
He'll say, "You're home; you're free."

Then my heart will leap with joy
As I look into His face.
He will draw me close to Him
He'll say, "You've won your race."

The glory and the beauty
That I'll behold with heavenly eyes,
Far exceeds the comprehension
Of anything I can surmise.

All of this and so much more,
Awaits as I onward go
Upon my earthly journey
Until I reach my heavenly home.

Chapter 9

"OUR WORLD" TORN APART

The room was quiet, very quiet. "Duane, how are you doing today?" asked our friend and counselor, Dr. Earl Henslin, who often came to give us support and comfort. Today was different, however. Earl had come to help us deal with harder things. It was now nine months since we'd been told by Dr. Ovando that Duane was terminal.

The tears were flowing to the point that it was hard to breathe. I felt like I was drowning in my own tears. My heart ached until it felt like a heart attack was in progress. Maybe it was. My emotional being was so fragmented that my whole body was numb.

Hard questions were on my mind:

- "God, where is Your mercy?
- Where is Your comfort?
- Why haven't You answered our prayers?"

I kept asking my questions as the tears continued to flow.

For days, we watched Duane slowly lose his battle with cancer. What made it even more grueling was that we were trying to cope with so many things. We were trying to walk through physical pain and isolation because of his ear problems. We were trying to get our equilibrium back as we dealt with Tammie's death and the four divorces. With Duane's declining health and physical needs, it was hard to hang onto the "JOY OF THE LORD." It seemed like trying to mix oil and water. But we both tried!

"Duane, how do you feel about going to heaven soon?" Through a fog, I heard Duane's voice reply weakly, "I'm ready, Earl. My concern is for Carole. Would you check on her once in a while to see how she is doing?" That was so like my beloved; to be more concerned for me than for himself. I loved that man so much. I wondered how could I ever live without him, yet at the same time, I knew I could not bear to keep watching his suffering. At some point, I had to let go of him. Sometime I had to say, "Honey, it is okay for you to go to be with Jesus. I'll be all right because the Lord will take care of me just like He took care of both of us and our family through the years."

Earl suddenly stepped aside and motioned for me to take his place beside the bed. To my dread, I knew that the time had arrived. The necessary words came out of my mouth as I confidently held Duane's hand; tears ran down both our cheeks. This confidence could only have come from the Lord since I was beyond controlling my emotional state. We talked about heaven and those he would see there and what he would do. We also talked about how wonderful it would be to see the Jesus face-to-face; to see Duane's parents; both of our oldest granddaughters would be there to greet him. In fact, we counted more people of our family in heaven than here on earth. I told him I was praying for angels to fill our bedroom because I wanted him to tell me how beautiful they were. When we were through, Earl came closer to the bed; we all held hands and prayed together.

It was then that I slipped away to the bathroom for a long moment to gather my emotions. Once again, a river of tears began to flow and I shook with emotion. I still had questions on my lips, and I began quietly pouring out my heart out to the Lord. I did not want Duane to see me in this condition, nor anyone else for that matter. After all, it was all he could do to just keep alive. He was seldom out of bed now. The bathroom seemed my only hiding place to grieve. I often cried out to the Lord behind this closed door or in closets, in the car, on walks or in any secluded place I could find. Wiping away the tears, I finally opened the bathroom door.

I tried to keep the worst of my suffering from my family and closest friends. But they knew … and they prayed for both of us. All the cards, the flowers, and the calls that came revealed this.

There was an army of Christian friends who held us before the Throne of Grace on a daily basis. Some of those dear people we did not know, but they helped us carry our burdens. Some of these people were even from other countries. This spoke volumes to us. It seemed the Lord was saying, " I know, I care, and I AM with you!"

It became evident to both Duane and me that we could no longer physically fight this battle of cancer without help. I made a trip to the office of our family doctor, Royce Hutain, and he gave me a referral for in-home Hospice care.

On November 21, 1997, we began this new challenge and met our Hospice Care Team. Duane was assigned very special people who were daily to walk with us, pray with us and not only care for Duane's physical needs, but for both of us in our spiritual and emotional needs, as well. Matt

Hillery was Duane's RN. He was a godly man who worked hard and long, spending countless hours using his skills as a nurse to make Duane as comfortable as possible. His time of prayer was always a strengthening factor. Obdulia Carbajal was Duane's daily caregiver. Her compassion for the sick was evident because of her loving ways shown to all of us. Many mornings she left her work shift with tears in her eyes. Kathy Perry came weekly to talk about any problems we might be dealing with. She guided us as a family through hard stressful times. She not only cared for all of us, but laughed with us as well.

Several days later, I called my sister-in-law Margie Hutchins in North Carolina and asked her to come. She had offered to live with us and help in any way that she could. She arrived within days of the call to share the cooking responsibilities, to answer the telephone and the door, to run errands, and to help with Duane's needs. Our bedroom became the focal point of our daily activities. The three of us had our meals together there. My other sister-in-law, Carol Schumacher, visited often and brought meals to lighten our load or to stay with Duane so we could run errands.

The Hospice team was in and out on a daily basis. After being isolated for nine years, it was hard to adjust to all that was going on. I even had dreams of people coming in through the windows and of telephones that never stopped ringing. Sleep, for me, became sporadic and my nerves became frayed.

I am a perfectionist by nature, and all of life seemed out of control. I did crazy things like trying to drive my car through a closed metal door, or starting out in the car to run an errand and ending in some unrelated place. As Duane's health declined in the next ten weeks, the boys started taking turns staying through the week. One of them was with us all the time. The last ten days, the family members took turns in two-hour shifts around the clock to be with Duane.

My precious parents (both in their late 80's) brought food, as did other family members, friends and neighbors. Dad had just finished his second hospitalization, taking chemotherapy for the cancer battle he was fighting, and yet he was right in there, doing his part to help.

God gave each of us a personal, private time with Duane and each of us was able to say our good-bye to him. We all felt that, as a family, this was a blessed privilege and a time that was precious to all of us.

In Duane, we saw a man who never wavered in his faith nor in his love for any of us or for his Lord. He still could smile and be appreciative of anyone who cared for him.

It was on Sunday morning, February 22, 1998 at 6:15 A.M. that my beloved husband went home to be with Jesus. He was at last free from his suffering. His was free from a body that held him a prisoner for so many years. We, as a family, were in deep sorrow but not like those who have no hope. We will be with him again.

Safely Home[1]

I am now at home in heaven;
All's so happy, all so bright!
There is perfect joy and beauty
In this everlasting light

All the pain and grief are over,
Every restless tossing past;
I am now at peace forever,
Safely home in heaven at last.

Did you wonder I so calmly
Trod the Valley of the Shade?
Oh! But Jesus' love illuminated
Every dark and fearful glade.

And He came Himself to meet me
In that way so hard to tread;
And with Jesus' arm to lean on,
Could I have one doubt or dread?

Then you must not grieve so sorely,
For I love you dearly still;
Try to look beyond earth's shadows,
You can trust our Father's will.

There is work still waiting for you,
So you must not idly stand;
Do your work while life remaineth –
You shall rest in Jesus' land.

When that work is all completed
He will gently call you home;
Oh, the rapture of that meeting!
Oh, the joy to see you come!

---

[1] American Tract Society, Box 462008, Garland, TX 75046.

* * * * *

Precious in the sight of the Lord
is the death of His saints.
Psalm 116:16

Jesus said, "Because I live,
ye shall live also."
John 14:19

And so shall we ever be with the Lord.
I Thessalonians 4:17

Cancer is a cruel disease. It is a robber of life—a robber of the quality of life; however, there are some things that cancer canot touch. Dr. Charles Swindoll wrote:

"Cancer is limited.
It cannot cripple love.
It cannot erode faith.
It cannot eat away peace.
It cannot destroy confidence.
It cannot kill friendships.
It cannot shut out our memories.
It cannot silence courage.
It cannot invade the soul.
It cannot reduce eternal life.
It cannot quench the Spirit.
It cannot lessen the power of the Resurrection."[2]

---

[2] Charles Swindoll; *The Finishing Touch*; © 1994; Word Publishing, Dallas, London, Vancouver, Melbourne; pg. 119.

I still miss my sweetheart of forty-eight years. I still cry, but not as much as I used to because I rejoice with Duane that he is in a much better place—heaven!

"He fought the good fight;

he finished the race;

he kept the faith."

II Timothy 4:7[3]

---

[3] Other comforting verses: Revelation 4:13, John 11:25, John 14:2, Philippians 1:21, Romans 10:13, II Corinthians 5:8.

Chapter Ten

Red Roses

SWEETHEARTS

We met while in our High School days,
I was ahead by two years.
We were drawn to one another by chance,
While we were leading cheers.

Our dates were off and on at first
But as time went by,
I realized that she was truly my choice
To love until I die.

With graduations behind us both,
I placed a ring upon her finger.
We were convinced beyond a doubt,
That wedding plans should not linger.

So the date was set and plans were made,
To exchange our vows at the altar.
We knew it was God's plan for us,
This conviction would never falter.

Time has flown by and a family's been raised,
The path strewn with joy and tears,
The commitment we made at the altar that day,
Tho' tested, has grown with the years.

Fifty years soon will have passed,
And yet we've not been apart.
It's God's gift to make two people one
And it's only found in the heart.

Duane D. Logsdon

Chapter 10

RED ROSES

This morning was different. Already the sun was coming through the bedroom windows; it looked hot outside and it was warm inside.

Opening my eyes from a hard night's sleep, my thoughts turned to the date, August 26, 1949. Overwhelming loss of Duane hurt like a knife cutting into flesh. My memory could feel his touch, an engulfing hug and kiss. I could hear his words of endearment. In reality, I was alone in my bed, in a room surrounded by heavy silence. I felt abandoned. Today would have been our 49th wedding anniversary.

As I rolled over in bed, I came face to face with my beloved's picture on the wall and I whispered, "Happy anniversary, Honey." It was then that the tears came in a flood. It seemed my broken heart was open for the world to see.

The morning passed slowly. I knew Duane would not want me to spend the day with tears and depression, so I wanted to make plans to do something positive with all of these mixed emotions. I knew it would help to do something with someone else. Calls were made to three special girlfriends—Bonnie Morris, Midge Finley, Betty Jacobs. They all knew what it was to be alone. Reservations were made for the four of us at 7:30 P.M. at a very nice local restaurant, The Cat and The Custard Cup. I appreciated their taking time out of their busy schedules. Duane and I would have celebrated had he been there, and he would have approved of this. After all, where he was, was better than being here on earth, but this was the best I could do. After watching all of his suffering, I did not want him back to suffer more, and I was happy for him that he was with his Lord. Bonnie, Midge and Betty have walked with me—praying, encouraging and listening to my cries of hurt and loneliness. Their patience has been displayed by their love, concern and by their not giving up on me. I wanted to share this evening with them.

After making the dinner arrangements, my thoughts returned to past anniversaries. Last year, Duane had written a poem for me. It was a gift from his heart and it became one of my greatest treasures. Some of Duane's poems are so personal they were not meant to be shared. With shaking hands, I reached for the poetry book he worked on during the last two years of his life. This book had been untouched for six months. I could still see him sitting in the living room chair with pen and paper in hand, thinking and writing— often talking, reading his words out loud. This was his chair, his quiet corner, the place where he read his Bible and talked things over with the Lord. The first few months after his death, I could not bring myself even to look at the now empty place. Today, though, I wanted to open the book and look at the empty chair. I wanted the intimate privilege of remembering him as my husband, God's gift for my life.

August Twenty-Sixth

Of all the months of the calendar year,
August can surely boast.
In August, wonderful things took place;
I remember them the most.

On the twenty-first day, you were born,
Your whole family rejoiced with joy.
You grew up to become a beautiful girl;
I'm so glad you weren't a boy.

As we dated, I soon realized that
I wanted you as my wife.
Somehow I felt you were God's choice
To live with the rest of my life.

You've given me 48 wonderful years;
My love has grown deeper each one.
Thanks for the way you've given yourself.
I'm richer for all that you've done.

Love,
Buddy 1997

I think most couples that are close have pet names for each other. Through the years, I gave Duane several ... my Buddy, my Precious, my Prince. He truly had treated me like a princess for more than forty-eight years.

All those years, at some time on this day, I received a dozen red roses from him. However, today the doorbell would not ring. There would be no more roses. Trying to pull myself into the "present" and the "positive," I reminded myself how wonderful it was that I had wonderful memories of the man who loved me, who wrote poetry for me. He was the man who stole my heart and became my life. Now, it was my turn to give him roses.

It was late morning, and the car seemed to drive by itself to La Petite Florist Shop in Brea, California. I had been there several times buying flowers and was always received with personal kindness and professionalism by the staff. The flowers were not only fresh but the arrangements were beautifully done. They had done two baskets of red roses for Duane's Celebration of Life Service that was held at the First Evangelical Free Church of Fullerton where we attended for many years. Somehow, I linked them to this expression of love. After our greeting, I told them why I had come and that I wanted one dozen red roses for the receptacle at the cemetery. On my way out, one of the staff, a small lady, pulled two big, beautiful carnations from a large vase and said, "Honey, these are for you." Somehow, I felt she identified with my pain and the difficulty of this day. This was her way of offering me comfort. I thanked her and left.

In the few blocks from the flower shop to the cemetery, the feeling of grief and sorrow seemed to change to one of peace and strength. The car seemed filled with the presence of the Lord. This time was special ... I was not alone after all.

Later that day, a fax came from a very special friend of our family, Dr. Darrell Countryman. I so appreciated the encouragements of his comments:

> *"You seem to be pacing yourself quite well in your grieving. Your conscious level is consumed with daily responsibilities and mixed emotions about heavy burdens. Meanwhile there are slow changes taking place on the unconscious level. The Holy Spirit who weeps when you weep, and laughs when you laugh, directs those changes. What's more, He presents your every need to the Father, every day. He also goes with you to the cemetery when you talk and remember."*

As I placed the roses in the container full of water, I talked to Duane and to the Lord. It was with a thankful heart that I expressed my gratitude to my wonderful Savior for giving me such a wonderful mate. Duane was a godly man with integrity and concern for others, and that was a gift to me, too. I thanked the Lord for His plan, and asked Him that, whatever His plan had been for Duane and me as a couple, He would give me the strength and wisdom to be able to carry it out for His honor and His glory. The day was spent in reflection of past memories; now it was time to make a new memory.

The dining room was filled with happy noises, music, and happy people all around us enjoying one another. There was a beautiful lamp on the table surrounded by colorful china and color-coordinated napkins. As Bonnie, Midge, Betty and I laughed and made plans for an Anaheim Angel's baseball game, we each spoke of a memorable time that we had shared with our husbands. We made a toast—"To beautiful past memories, and to the present, and to the future for the making of new memories."

After coming home and walking into the bedroom, it seemed as though Duane were there and happy with the positive things that had occupied "Our Day." With peace in my heart I said, "Goodnight sweetheart, I'll always love you!"

The things learned this day had been many. Here's a note from one of Chuck Swindoll's messages from Insight for Living. I noted it in my Bible since it meant so much to me. For anyone who walks down the path of grief and sorrow it is truthful to say:

- We are loved by the Lord, even when we don't feel like it
(KEEP FAITHFUL).

- We are never alone
(KEEP COMMUNICATING WITH HIM. DON'T GIVE UP).

- We still have a life to live, even in our sorrow and grief
(KEEP LOOKING UP).

Chapter Eleven

Love in Transition

WE'LL UNDERSTAND

When the pieces of life's puzzle finally fall in place,
And the answers to my questions fully told;
Things that seem unjust, unfair,
Will turn out to be treasures of gold.

All the pain and trials that we could not understand
Came from God. We knew He loved us so.
He'll reveal that His wonderful plan,
Needed testings that would help us to grow.

Our Lord will explain as He looks in our eyes,
He'll unfold mysteries—the cause of our doubt.
He wrote in His Word which we've read many times,
"My ways are not yours, they're past finding out."

Oh! The gratitude and praise that will come from within!
We'll fall at His feet and adore.
By His love and His grace we came through the fire
To reign with Him forevermore.

Duane D. Logsdon

Chapter 11

LOVE IN TRANSITION

Love shared.

Love lost.

Love in transition.

It all means change.

When a permanent change comes into our life, there is a personal battle to accept that change. The fight takes place in our emotions and in our mind. There is resistance, an inner turmoil, tears all mixed up in our prayers for the Lord's grace, mercy and help. Whatever the cause of change, these experiences bring us to moments of decision. This is not a one-time commitment but an on-going, daily, minute-by-minute experience.

For weeks, there had been a void in my life, an emptiness, a hole that seemed never to get filled. I shrugged it off as normal for one being in grief. To accept it and live with it was heaviness to my soul.

- What is wrong?
- What am I feeling?
- What transitions need to be addressed?
- What are my choices?

It was one o'clock in the morning as I turned on the light and reached for the book, *"Edges Of His Ways,"*[1] by Amy Carmichael. Turning to the devotional for the day, these words seemed to minister to my heart with keen awareness:

"No single one of the circumstances (of life) has any power in itself to upset ***the joy of God,*** *but it can instantly and utterly quench it if we look at the circumstances instead of looking up into the Face of light and love that is looking down upon us—the Face of our own God. This is the shining path, stretching away from the place where we stand today to the very heart of God. This is the shining path that shineth more and more as we walk in it."*

The words, *"joy of God"* seemed to stand out. It was for sure that my circumstances and feelings were far from being joyful ... but there was more. I was in transition and the Lord was teaching me about His love, a dimension in depth that I had not yet reached. After praying and asking the Lord what He was telling me, it seemed evident that I would not know the joy of my God until I had faced the issue of the "love of my God."

This transition seemed to be moving from a visible, hands-on, heart-related relationship with my husband to an invisible faith walk—a love walk with my Lord. It seemed to make sense. It not only made me look upward but inward as well. This walk is a deeper dimension of love that in some ways I did not want and yet I was pushed by

---

[1] *Edges Of His Ways;* C 1955, Dohnavur Fellowship, First American Edition 1975; Christian Literature Crusade, Box 1449, Fort Washington, Pennsylvania, 19034; pg. 127.

desperation to accept it. There seemed to be no choice in the matter; that is, there were none if I wanted to grow and get beyond my grief. It became evident that peace and joy would not come to me until I settled with Him this matter of faith —the "evidence of things not seen."

Letting go of the tangible for the intangible was like jumping off of a cliff. I still wanted to cling to the old ways of expression and love, the ways of solving the daily problems as a couple with the Lord. This was a relationship that I could see, feel, and depend upon. It was a relationship that was visible and comforting. Duane was my earthly joy, my life. Now the Lord was beckoning me to walk deeper into His love and care. Would I be willing?

I argued with the Lord in prayer, reminding Him that He was my Savior and my Lord. We had gone through this before on other occasions. It seemed He was saying, "But I want to be more to you; trust Me." After several days of this struggle, my daily Bible reading took me to Isaiah 54:4-6:

> "*...the sorrows of widowhood will be remembered no more, for your creator will be your 'husband.' The Lord almighty is his name; he is your Redeemer, the Holy One of Israel the God of all the earth. For the Lord has called you back from your grief....*"

This unrest of soul and the spurning of His love tore me apart. Again I read, "[My] ***creator*** will be [my] ***husband.*** the ***Lord almighty***..., [my] ***Redeemer,*** the ***Holy One of Israel***, the ***God of all the earth." He is the One*** who calls me back from my grief. ***He is the ONE*** who promises to be my husband.

Did this mean that I would not feel the stabbing pains of grief again or know the tearing emotions and loss that comes with death? No, because we all face disappointments and loss for one reason or another. It's called life! ***This experience meant a more intimate, personal relationship of love with my Savior, my Lord, and now my "husband."***

Through the years, it had been Duane's walk with the Lord, and how he treated me and loved me, that paved the way for my personal fellowship with the Lord. Until I reached the age of twenty-one, I saw God as a superior, powerful Being with a big stick. This superior Being was awesome but unapproachable to meet any of my needs. At the same time, in spite of fearing His wrath, there was something that pulled me closer to Him. The Lord used Duane as the living example of how to deal with that apparent contradiction. After our conversion, our marriage was based on I Corinthians 11: 3 (KJV):

> "*But I want you to know the head of every man is Christ, the head of woman is man, the head of Christ is God.*"

This did not mean that I was inferior or subservient to Duane in any way. It did not mean that I should not exercise my own judgment or that I was to be his slave. We were partners. I had important responsibilities, just as he had. We worked together; we listened to each other. This verse was a code of respect for one another that the Lord put in His Word for our happiness and success. It was given to remind us that we were both accountable to God for the way we treated each other. We both worked hard at keeping our relationship right before God. Duane was the head of our home. He also took I Peter 3:7 (KJV) seriously,

> "*Likewise you husbands dwell with them (wives) with understanding, giving honor to the wife, as to the weaker vessel, as* ***being heirs together*** *of the grace of life, that your prayers may not be hindered.*"

Caring for each other with respect was a big part of the foundation of our marriage.

Up until now, my needs had been met by our earthly love and together we experienced the spiritual, soul love of the Lord. Now my needs had changed. Duane was gone and I found myself face-to-face with Jesus, envisioning Him standing before me with open arms. He was no longer the awesome Being with a big stick. I wanted more than anything to run into His arms of love, to trust Him, to commune with Him and to adore my Heavenly Bridegroom.

It was then that I was able to pray, "Oh Lord, please forgive my insensitivity and coldness toward Your deep love. Please forgive my lack of submission to the most intimate of spiritual relationships. Please forgive my pulling away from You instead of running into Your arms. Loss and grief have left deep scars in my life. But Lord, You bore the scars of love in Your body that are far greater than mine. Someday I will be able to witness those scars of love with my own eyes and fall at Your feet in worship and adoration. Thank You for Your promises of care and love. Thank You for Your patience while I am learning. Thank

You for Your *'treasures that are hidden in the darkness'* and for Your secret riches. They are unending. My heart is full; words cannot express my joy."

It is God who initiated the intimacy I enjoyed with my husband. It is God who has initiated His spiritual intimacy with me and who said He would be my husband. My heart was flooded with His love.

When I finished typing the prayer as I wrote this chapter, the telephone rang. There had been a crisis in my life with estate matters and cash flow problems. This had consumed my energy and my peace. Yes, I prayed, but God did not seem to be answering. These were problems that Duane would have handled with ability, wisdom and strength. Just now, all these qualities were lacking in my life. At times, it was overwhelming to cope with these things. I had been in and out of depression; I was eating and sleeping with no set routine. It was easy to run from sun up until sun down. Keeping busy dulled the pain. Even meals were eaten standing up or on the run. My close friends were aware of my up and down days. These experiences were all a part of the grief experience; also, they were part of my learning to cope in the business world. Daily I cried to the Lord to make up for my ever-present deficiencies.

"Hello, Carole. This is Susan (my attorney). I am so happy to be able to bring you good news for a change. Your prayers have been answered."

A financial crisis had been met. I couldn't help but notice the timing of these answers to prayer. With thanksgiving in my heart, I opened my Bible and read Isaiah 45.3 (LB):

"And I will give you ***treasures hidden in the darkness,*** *secret riches, and you will know that I am doing this—I, the Lord, the God of Israel, the one who calls you by your name."*

Again I went back to Isaiah 54:4-6 (LB):

"The sorrows of widowhood will be remembered no more, for your creator will be your 'husband.' The Lord Almighty is his name; he is your Redeemer, the Holy One of Israel, the God of all the earth. For the Lord has called you back from your grief."

Chapter Twelve

Jenae, My Gift

LORD TAKE MY HAND

Lord, take my hand.
Lead me on my journey.
I'm but a child
And could easily lose my way.
You take the lead,
Then I'll know that You are with me
I'll follow close;
Behind You, I will stay.

Lord, take my hand.
Protect me from temptations
That lay hidden
Along life's narrow way
So I by chance will not wander
Like wayward sheep
Who often go astray.

Lord, take my hand..
Help me through the trials
That You have said
Will surely come to pass.
Help me rise
Above each one in victory,
And count them joy
Until I'm home at last.

Duane D. Logsdon

Chapter 12

JENAE, MY GIFT

"Hey Gram, I just met a new friend. She is staying with her grandmother, too. And you know what? Her parents are getting a divorce too. We had a lot to talk about."

For the next three weeks, Jenae and her friend met at the pool. They talked, they played tennis together in the evenings, ate meals together, and went to movies. This relationship started a conversation between Jenae and me on a topic that we had not discussed before—not at any personal depth anyway. We started talking about the emotional trauma of a family when there is a divorce. So we got the bright idea to do something with pictures. We hunted up old magazines, or anything with pictures or print that we could tear apart or cut out. We were hunting for pictures that portrayed the feelings that we talked about.

Magazines were everywhere. There was the sound of scissors cutting paper, the tearing of scotch tape, paper flying all over the floor, and an air of excitement in the room as we found something that we could use. Our project was to make a collage of feelings. Words, pictures—anything we could find to express our feelings— were cut out and taped onto typing paper. It was an art project of self-expression about our thoughts. This opened up very serious conversation about topics we had never discussed before—divorce and death. We cried together, laughed together and shared funny pictures as well as sad ones. Sometimes we laughed so hard the tears rolled down our cheeks.

She was only eleven years old, but wise beyond her years. She had already known heartache in her life, deep heartache. She knew about divorce and its pain, from a child's point of view. She knew about loss, not only through divorce but also through several forms of hurt and disappointment: She walked with a best friend whose brother killed himself. She walked by my side when "Grandpa" was sick and went home to be with Jesus. We sat side by side at the graveside and at the Celebration of Life Service. She walked with her Mommie through the illness of cancer and several surgeries.

These experiences have made her stronger in character and in her love for Jesus than she ever could have been without them. However, she does have questions. So do I, but then Job didn't know about the conversation that God had with the Devil, either. Job knew **by faith** that God would someday make known to him the "why" of all of his troubles.

The Lord has given Jenae special insight into His love for her. She walks with Him and talks to Him with great freedom, and she doesn't blame the Lord for her experiences in life. I'm proud to be her Grandmother!

Amy Carmichael put it this way:

> We often think of life under the form of picture words. Life is a fight, a wrestle, a journey, a race, a climb, and so on. This morning I was thinking of it as a voyage, with no promise of calm seas. Then I

came upon this in Psalm 89:9, "'*When the waves, arise, Thou stillest them.*"[1]

Jenae was a gift to me that summer. She taught me many things about what the Lord can do with a life, a young life...even an older life when it is reeling with feelings of loss and disappointment. She taught me how to laugh again; to feel alive again. The miracle of her attitude gave me a glimpse of a brighter side of life. We've laughed a lot, played a lot (even golf), and (like most females) we've shopped a lot and we've talked a lot. Soul talk!

We had yet another experience of life to walk through. Great Grandpa Wayne was also battling cancer—brain cancer. We came home from the desert house to be with him and Nee Nee (my mother). Grandpa Wayne was 83 years old and Nee Nee was 86 years old. We knew there would be more losses down the road. It had only been a few months since Jenae and I sat side by side at her other Grandpa's funeral. That same day, her mother went back into the hospital again.

How do you explain all of this to a child of eleven? Where do we go for comfort? We can only go to God's Word and apply the verses He has already given us and get a glimpse of the bigger picture. For some reason known only to Him, we have been asked to walk this pathway for His honor and glory. There is a purpose but we will probably not know what it is until we see Him face to face.

---

[1] *Edges Of His Ways*, Amy Carmichael; © 1955 Dohnavur Fellowship, 1995; Christian Literature Crusade; Box 1449, Fort Washington, Pennsylvania 19034; pg.98.

- There is comfort in the Lord because He will never leave us nor forsake us (Heb. 13:5).

- There is comfort in knowing our Father has sent His Comforter to us in our time of need (II Cor. 1:3,4,7,8).

- There is comfort in knowing that He will not test us beyond what we can endure (II Cor. 10:13).

- There is comfort in knowing that Jesus died for our sins and is preparing a place for us in Heaven (John 14:1-3).

- There is comfort in knowing that He is our strength and by His Grace we can live for Him and glorify Him even when life doesn't go as we would like (II Cor. 12:9).

Children hurt terribly when they are forced to accept the divorce of their parents. They are often lost in the shuffle between fighting parents. They learn by example how to hate or how to be peacemakers. They feel the responsibility to keep parents together and they feel guilt, blaming themselves for the problems. They learn anger, fear, denial, shame, loneliness, and blame. The list goes on and on.

Elaine Seppa, in her book, *When Your Children Divorce,*[2] mentions the long term effects that often result from divorce:

> Divorce doesn't stop taking its toll after two years, or when a child turns eighteen, or when the child marries and sets up a new home. Often I have heard adults say things like this:
>
> - "There was no dad when I was growing up, so I have trouble relating to men—I have trouble trusting them."
> - "I've looked for love in all the wrong places, not having strong guidance from an involved father."
> - "Mom was so busy trying to survive that she had little time for us. She was always tired."
> - "There was little joy at home. I left as soon as I possibly could."

Many children of divorced parents have known more than two sets of parents; they often have two bedrooms, two sets of interests on weekends (usually those interests are the parents' interests, not the child's). They can also be inundated with things to do and places to go. Buying children's love or making them slaves to the rights of

---

[2] *When Your Children Divorce*, Elaine R. Seppa; © 1995 InterVarsity Press; Downers Grove, IL 60515.

parents causes deep resentment when those children become adults. They end up having no childhood to speak of. Some learn early how to make a single parent feel guilty and they become the instrument of more turmoil in the family. Oftentimes, this is the result of failure in the parent's second marriage. It is "get-even" time. They come to believe that life and people owe them anything they want. Our society is full of examples of what young people do to get what they want. Sometimes one wonders who the victims really are. All we have to do is read the local newspaper for examples.

Some children face problems of another kind. They face abandonment and hardships of many kinds. Many of these children suffer extreme abuse and cruelty. They are young people set adrift on the sea of adult life...they either sink or swim.

Without being trained by examples of love and integrity, they often recreate the atmosphere they grew up in and repeat the behaviors that were modeled for them by the adults in their lives. Because of divorce and compounded problems, many grandparents or other family members are called upon to raise these children. This creates another set of problems. The courts may even assign visiting privileges to a parent that children do not want to be with. They learn to cope any way they can. Dr. James Dobson in *Children at Risk*, the book he co-authored with Gary Bauer, says, "More than one million children are affected by divorce every year. Mates are traded in for newer models as if they were cars."[3]

One young person of Jr. High School age, was asked how he felt about peer pressure after experiencing the divorce of his parents. He said, "Oh, its okay, most of my friends' parents are divorced anyway. Their parents work so we have a lot of homes to hang out in. Just being together is what counts. Sometimes we just hang out at the mall or bomb around in cars. We don't really care where we are." Some parents of these children don't even know where they are at night. All they have to say is, "I stayed with so and so" or they don't question them at all.

Many young people find friends on the Internet who will listen. Many times these are not the most desirable of counselors and some of them mean harm to our children.

The divorce of your adult children often puts grandparents in a new role where they do not know how to cope. Holidays, birthdays and parties can become a nightmare as we must ask who goes where, when is it OK for them to go?

What to do with previous family portraits (the ones that used to hang on the walls) are now hidden in the attic or buried in some inconspicuous closet. Your grandchildren see these come down as well.

The insecurity of our adult children and their new mates about your relationship with the ex-daughter-in-law

---

[3] *Children at Risk* Dr. James Dobson, Gary L. Bauer; © 1990: Word Publishing Co., Dallas, London, Vancouver, Melbourne, and printed in the USA.

or ex-son-in-law, can create many misunderstandings. Just because the parents have animosities doesn't mean the grandparents have them. There is always a tug of war for the children because they love both parents.

It also makes it hard on the children when one parent is not on civil or on speaking terms (even in public situations) with their ex-mates. The majority of young people feel like someone has to be protected but they stow the pain and walk on eggshells along with everyone else. It complicates life for the grandparents in a major way as we often wonder where and how we fit in. "Fitting in" is not always a possibility even though we try hard. This also affects the grandchild of divorced parents. They not only learn to stifle feelings but they learn, by example, an attitude of hate and criticism.

Some young people get so tired of walking the tight line that they just leave to get away from it all. There are more than a few grandparents who have had to visit their grandchildren in state institutions of correction. The grandchildren are so angry about being ripped off by their parents that they choose not to be accountable to anyone, themselves or society.

They see it as another "get-even" time without even realizing it. No one wins that game. Other young people side with one parent and refuse to have anything to do with the other for the rest of their life. Anger, resentment and rebellion can become lifetime scars. Sometimes the price of divorce is very high.

There are some parents who are divorced and yet they make the best of a bad situation. They love their children enough to spare them as much heartache as possible. Their homes are divided but without ugly attitudes and audible fighting, hatefulness and backbiting. There is still respect for all concerned. The parents still speak with their ex-spouses and work together as much as possible for the sake of their children.

Jenae and I talked about these things as we cut and pasted. She wanted to write a paragraph about each of the pages. As I close this chapter with *her words*, I'm sure you will come to the conclusion that young people have feelings and that they hurt just like adults when there is death or divorce in a family. And yet, some young people can have a very mature attitude about their circumstances and make positive goals for their own future regardless of how they have been hurt. Jenae wrote:

DEATH

"To me divorce and death are the hardest pains to cope with, but in a way they are the same because you feel the loss and emptiness of having to do without that person's presence. Although you know the Lord has a plan for all people, you still ask why He allowed that person to go. To me, it felt odd that when I went to that person's home. It felt as if he were there, even though I knew that he was not. My grandfather suffered for nine years and I was happy when he went home to heaven even though I was terribly sad. He was only gone two weeks and I felt as if it had been fifty years.

DIVORCE

"For most kids divorce is hard. It causes anger and hardship in most homes. Most times there is a strong pain in the child's heart that makes him feel unwanted or guilty. It makes kids emotionally shy because they feel other kids will tease them or make fun of them because they are different. Some kids cry themselves to sleep every night wanting to know why such a tragedy hit their home and tore their family in two. They fear one parent will fight for custody or take things to other drastic measures. Although I mention these things, it doesn't mean they happen in all homes. I thank the Lord that my parents still have a love and respect for one another.

GOD

"God has helped me through this more than anyone I know. I feel a desire in my heart when my grandmother cries, to be strong and help her any way I can. I try my hardest to keep steady, but eventually I give in and my tears roll like a storm. Oftentimes, when I pray to Jesus, I sleep better at night because He comforts me. I know He has given me the strength to get through it."

Chapter Thirteen

New Relationships

HIS GIFTS

Every day when we awake
It's a gift from God above.
He freely gives us to all of us
For we are objects of His love.

He sends the sunshine and the rain
To care for all He's made.
He gives us life, supplies our needs
And says, "Don't be afraid."

The world is His, He's in control
Though trials come our way.
His Word is true; He'll see us through
To live another day.

He asks that we will call on Him,
Accept salvation free;
Which He provides through Christ His Son
Who died at Calvary.

Duane D. Logsdon

Chapter 13

NEW RELATIONSHIPS

Our family seemed to be changing very quickly. We had been hurt by the divorces and now we had to prepare for new relationships. My mind went through frightening thoughts. What would our new daughters-in-law have in common with us? What experiences had we gone through in the past that would make us cautious, even distant? Would we ever blend into a new family?

Thinking about these relationships, my mind went through all the introductions that I could imagine. This was crazy stuff and we knew it would take time and consideration and the giving of love to build new relationships. It seemed all of us were ready to go on with life and get the hurts behind us, but the fear of the unknown was very present.

I could imagine hearing, "I would like you to meet my mother-in-law, Carole, the old bag I've been telling you about—the intruder, the controller, the whiner, the religious freak, the encourager, my other mother."

We hear a lot of "mother-in-law" jokes. Somehow the father-in-law doesn't seem to evoke the same images. How many books have you ever read on this subject or heard of counseling courses offered? Most of the time it is a trial-and-error experience. We aren't given a set of rules to go by when we first enter into an "in-law" relationship, only examples. I am not so sure that many new mothers-in-law would follow them anyway because we have preconceived ideas about what we want to be and what we should expect out of the relationship. We want the best for our children and yet when do you stop parenting?

My mother-in-law was a very caring and beautiful person. I knew nothing of the domestic side of life and she was patient and helpful to me in so many ways. Never once did she give unasked for advice about anything. Yet, she was always available to be helpful and she loved to entertain. After I became a pastor's wife, she shared cooking and cleaning ideas, and filled our house with pictures and hand-painted items. She has gone on to be with the Lord but she will always be "My Other Mother."

Sometimes a parent can make or break the marriage of their children because they won't let go of their son or daughter, or they become too involved in their children's affairs.

Dr. Mark W. Lee in his book, *"Time Bombs in Marriage"* has a classic illustration taken from an Ann Landers article:

- When a son or daughter lets you know they plan to be married, show open hostility to the person of his choice. After all, marriage means less love and attention for the parents, and they have a right to be resentful.
- Expect your married children to spend every Sunday and every holiday at your home. Act hurt if they have other plans.
- If your married children have problems with their mates, encourage them to come home to you. Let them know your home is still their home, no matter what. Listen attentively to all

complaints and point out additional faults which may have gone unobserved. Remember, a drop of water at a time can even wear away a rock – if you keep at it long enough.

- If your married children are having financial problems, rush in with the checkbook. If you are having financial problems yourself, borrow, if necessary, but let them know they'll never have to do without anything as long as you are around.
- If your married child has a drinking problem, keep telling him his mate drove him to it. It will make him feel better. Everyone needs someone to blame.
- If your married child gets an opportunity for advancement which takes him to another city, tell him family is more important than money and if he leaves, God will punish him for not obeying the commandments, "Honor thy father and the mother" (or do the next best thing, follow him).
- If there are grandchildren, smother them with gifts. If the parents object, tell them to keep out of it. After all, grandchildren are to spoil. Sneak money to the kids secretly, if you have to. They'll love you for it.
- If your married child has a difference of opinion, get into the act and fan the flames. Family loyalty is a beautiful thing. Maybe you can turn

> a minor argument into a major hassle and break up the marriage.[1]

At this point, I felt like I had broken all the rules at some time or another.

What are some of the lessons in love that our children ask of us as parents?

- To love our adult children for who they are.
- Give them the privilege of sharing their lives with us from a proper and healthy distance.
- Give unconditional love.

For love is patient, kind, not envious or proud.
It isn't rude or self-seeking, isn't easily provoked
nor does it keep records of wrongs.
It rejoices with truth, protects,
trusts, hopes, and always perseveres.
I Cor. 13:3-7

This is quite a check list for any relationship and one that requires work on everyone's part. We are responsible for our own motives and behaviors. The problems come when we are not aware or do not want to recognize our own shortcomings, much less see any need to change them. This is why the Scriptures are like a mirror and only the Holy Spirit can reveal to our hearts what we are really like

---

[1] *Time Bombs in Marriage,* Mark W. Lee; © 1981; Christian Herald Books, 40 Overlook Dr., Chappaqua, N.Y. 10514; pp. 47,48.

on the inside. There is one hitch—you've got to want to know yourself and how you behave toward others.

Prove yourselves doers of the Word,
not merely hearers who delude themselves.

If one is a hearer of the Word and not a doer

he is like a man
who looks at his natural face in a mirror,

for once he has looked at himself and gone away,
he has immediately forgotten what kind of person he was.
James 1:22-24 (NAS)

We are continually in a pattern for growth and we will continue this until God is through with us here on earth. There is no perfection, **but love is the key to successful living.** Learning to love and be considerate of others is an ongoing choice.

To Renee, Jeri, Rosemary and Angie, I want to say, "Thank you for your patience with me as I learn again about being a mother-in-law. You are four lovely young women and I count it a privilege to have you as daughters. May our relationship be one of consideration, honesty and, most of all, one of unconditional love. May we be able to look back upon the years we have together and thank the Lord because we are blessed to be a family.

"Lord, as an older, new mother-in-law, let there be love and acceptance in our relationship. May there be understanding without competition. May there be consideration of each other in our daily experiences in life. Help us to be in tune with each other's hurts, healing and growth. Lord, help us not to expect perfection in each other. May we have respect in our differences. Keep our relationship from being idealistic in purpose, but real, sincere and honest. But most of all, Lord, let there be love."

Chapter Fourteen

A Song in the Night

AWAKENED

I dreamed the other night the rapture had occurred.
Believers were all with the Lord as He's told us in His Word.

Caught up with Him how wonderful! I could not comprehend.
The glory of it stretched beyond Imagination's power to transcend.

To finally be with Jesus was the grandest part of all.
To feel His presence, hear His voice; I was totally enthralled.

I looked at all the faces, there were many that I knew;
Folks I'd known from various places. They numbered more than a few.

I then searched for individuals, friends and others I had known.
I saw many, some I didn't see. I thought, "Surely they were His own."

Looking around for loved ones; I saw that most were there.
There were some I couldn't find, "Surely they're here, but where?"

Then I sought the Lord for them, mentioned each one by name.
His warm and loving eyes met mine, "I called them; they never came."

He softly, gently touched my face, lifting my sad eyes to His.
"We did the best we could. Now we'll eternally live."

With a start I was awake; relieved it was only a dream.
Determination filled my heart to pray for those I missed seeing.

To spend time with family and all my friends
Sharing thoughts eternal and free;
And to do everything within my power
That they may see Christ in me.

Duane D. Logsdon

Chapter 14

A SONG IN THE NIGHT

Water turned off?

Thermostat set?

Everything out in the house?

As we scurried out the door, Dad was audibly going through the checklist of closing up the house. Time was getting away from us, traffic-wise. Our goal was to hit the freeway traffic in the late morning in order to miss the morning L.A. gridlock. Going to Palm Desert, California, was in our favor, though, as traffic would be going into L.A., not away from it.

For Mom, Dad and myself, there were other concerns that troubled us more. Would Dad ever again return to his home in Brea, California? Had we taken the things he needed for his last few weeks or months with us? How would any of us face more patient care-taking responsibilities and emotional stress, so soon after Duane's homegoing? It had been ten months now since Duane's death and so much had happened. The last Christmas that Duane was with us, Dad was diagnosed with a reoccurrence of cancer. We all tried to cram into our lives every positive memory that God would allow. However, these times were between surgeries, chemotherapy, radiation treatments and days of emotional and physical struggle.

The day after Dad's last radiation treatment, the three of us boarded a plane for Amarillo, Texas. Dad wanted to see his family one more time; he had four brothers in their 90's and time wasn't standing still for any of them. Seeing them and their families once more would be such a gift to him. Mom and I wanted very much to see this dream come true. Now it was happening! Never before had Mom and I been so accepted and loved by a family as we were by the Reynolds family. There is something wonderful about their Texas hospitality, When they say, "Y'all come!" they really mean it. Each year the family has a reunion at the Ramada Inn East for everyone. They meet to have fun, to laugh and to share their year with young and old alike.

We asked for wheelchair assistance for Dad. Southwest Airline had everything in place for us. When we reached Phoenix for a layover things began to change, however. Dad wanted pancakes in the worst way so we headed for the food court. It was further away than any of us anticipated. About halfway there, I looked back to see how Mom was doing and she was no place in sight. After retracing our steps, I knew Mom could not make the rest of the trip without a wheelchair, too. Being 86 years old and having breathing difficulties, it was evident that we needed help even to get back to the boarding area, with or without pancakes.

Southwest again came to our rescue. They summoned a young man to bring another wheelchair, help with the pancakes, and to return us to the second boarding area. What an angel and what an answer to prayer.

We had another surprise when we landed in Amarillo. More help was waiting to get us into the terminal. There, in front, were Dad's three brothers, his niece and her husband and their grandchildren holding a big banner welcoming us to the Reynolds Reunion. I am sure this was not an everyday sight. Now we had five wheelchairs, a banner, plus a group of people to meet us. One passenger said, "The press should be here to see this!" We had to take three elevators to get everyone to the baggage claim department and out the door.

Six months later, Dad had lost a lot of ground. He was under Hospice care but he wanted to spend his remaining weeks or months in the desert.

The new Hospice nurses became the highlight of our day. Joan, Barbara and Donna worked hard to help us with Dad's daily care, medication and bandaging him after his many falls. There were emergencies, medication checks and talks about encouragement from which we all benefited. It wasn't long before 24-hour care was needed and Blanche Fresques became Dad's night nurse. Dad couldn't always remember "Blanche" so he called her "My girl."

All the while Mom and I cared for Dad, we were concerned whether or not (when the time came for Dad to leave us) he would be ready to meet the Lord. It was our constant prayer and concern.

Dad was a wonderful person, kind, loving, moral and thoughtful. Even with these wonderful traits of character, however, we were concerned that he did not know the Lord Jesus Christ as his personal Savior. I felt desperate for the Lord to use us, or to show us what to do, or to send someone to prepare Dad for this journey and give us peace about this matter. There had been talks for years but still there was a question in our minds. When asked if he knew the Lord, he would always reply, "Yes." The reason we were unsure is that we never heard him say that he knew or loved the Lord unless he was asked. Being shy about praying, he always asked Mom to pray. Pastor Buck Buchanan from my church, First Evangelical Free Church of Fullerton, California, visited him several times. Dad always welcomed Buck and appreciated his concern and prayers for him. However, since Dad was an authoritative retired Orange County Highway Patrolman, one never went beyond the Holy Spirit's leading in this matter.

This Sunday morning was different. The burden was very heavy on my heart. It seemed our prayers were not being heard, and time was getting short,

"Hey, what's going on in there?" Dad asked. "It's a surprise Dad, I'm going to give you a real professional foot bath and a pedicure." There was a long silence, He wasn't so sure if he wanted that or not!

As Dad sat in the wheelchair with his feet in the foot tub there was more silence. While I sat on the floor with towels all around, I just prayed that somehow Dad would see God's love for him. Then I heard him say, "Jesus is watching you." I said, "Yes, Dad, Jesus is watching all of us. Why did you say that?" "Well, this is Sunday and Jesus washed His disciples' feet."

> *Lord, thank you for hearing my prayer. Thank you for using a very small expression of love to cause Dad to think of You. Please reveal Your love and make Your presence known to him. Lord, is Dad ready for the transition from earth to Heaven? Has he accepted you as his Savior sometime in his early years? Please, Lord, if he hasn't made that decision, guide us through this most important time.*

There was a feeling of urgency the rest of the day. The burden seemed so heavy and time seemed so short. In fact, at the end of the day, I was beginning to feel the moment had passed for Dad and somehow I had missed it. There was a ritual to putting Dad to bed. When he felt up to it, he was the one who left us with a merry heart when we said good night.

As I pulled the chair up to Dad's bed, our conversation seemed led by the Lord when I asked him what went through his mind, knowing that he would soon face eternity. "You know, Dad, think of all of your family that is waiting for you in Heaven. You're the youngest of a family of brothers and sisters. Your little Mom is probably saying to us, 'Take care of my baby boy as he will soon be coming home.' Dad, at anytime in your life have you ever prayed with anyone or personally asked the Lord Jesus Christ to come into your heart and save you?" His answer was "No. Is that important?" "Dad, it is the most important decision you will ever make on earth. Would you like to do that right now?" "Well, I'm not good at praying; I don't know what to say. Would you help me?"

Through tears, Dad prayed after me:

> *Lord, I come to You tonight to invite You into my heart. I thank You for loving me and dying for me and forgiving my sins. Thank You for being with me and saving me.*

Dad was tiring, but we shared these Scriptures:

GOD'S LOVE:

"*God so loved the world, that he gave his only begotten Son, that whosoever believes in him should not perish, but have everlasting life*" (John 3:16).

GOD'S WAY:

"*I am the way, the truth, and the life: no man comes unto the Father, but by me*" (John 14:6).

GOD'S REWARD:

"*If we confess our sins, he is faithful and just to forgive us our sins, and to cleanse us from all unrighteousness.*" (I John 1:9).

"*Blessed be the God and Father of our Lord Jesus Christ, which according to his abundant mercy has caused us to be born again to a living hope through the resurrection of Jesus Christ from the dead, To an inheritance incorruptible, and undefiled, and that fadeth not away, reserved in heaven for you*" (I Peter 1: 3,4).

There was such rejoicing and tears!

Our song in the night came the following evening as Mom and I tucked Dad into bed and gathered on each side of him to have prayer. With heads bowed, in a very firm and, loud voice, we heard Dad say, "Father, thank you for your love, Thank you for hearing a beginner's prayer."

Little did we know that in a matter of a few days, Dad would see his blessed Lord face to face and know firsthand of that most important decision.

In five years, we have lost, in death, six members of our immediate family (Tammie, our granddaughter; Duane, my Sweetheart of 49 years; a very dear Aunt, Mom's sister; her husband, a very special Uncle; a niece and now Dad) and we have gone through the divorces of our four children. Life on earth seems so temporal and Heaven seems closer. I ask the Lord:

> *Father, how many do I come in contact with each day who don't know You? Use my life in any way that You see fit. Thank you for the wonderful gift of Dad Reynolds. The gifts that he gave to Mom and to me as we cared for him, especially, when we were so tired in body and discouraged in spirit that You gave us all such a wonderful song in the night—Dad's conversion.*

Chapter Fifteen

A Way Through the Wilderness

VICTORS

Have you wondered why He does not come?
When to Him you plead your pain?
Mary and Martha wondered, too,
But it appeared to be all in vain,

We're often puzzled by things not done,
That He seems to say He will do.
We fail to remember in our plight,
That He's with us, He just isn't through.

He has at heart His best for us,
Scripture tells us that it's true.
Someday the clouds will lift,
And the sun will then break through.

Till then my friend you must take heart,
For His work with you isn't done,
To His promises then hold fast and firm,
They declare that we have won.

Duane D. Logsdon

Chapter 15

A WAY THROUGH THE WILDERNESS

For several months after Dad Reynolds passed away life seemed unfair. Everything was negative and physical strength did not seem to match the everyday responsibilities.

My mental attitude was giving way to feelings of self-pity, the "poor-me" mentality. It wasn't long before depression took hold and there was a battle of battles to keep my faith. If there was a God, why would He allow so much emotional pain, confusion and hurt? It seemed everywhere I looked, loneliness was my shadow. That shadow filled my entire being with the same darkness. Even in the midst of a crowd, I was alone.

My family and my best friends could not touch my loneliness. How could they when I wouldn't even let the Lord into my life ... that close? That was evident by the experience in the prayer room at my church. It was unfair of me to criticize those who had come to help me. They were trying to comfort, but I did not want their suggestions, much less their advice—just their prayers. I wanted *them* to take away the pain … but God, in His love, would not allow that to happen. My Lord was standing before me, waiting with open arms. He wanted to be my comfort and my "ALL" but I was digging in my heels and yelling, "'No ... not this way Lord. DON'T WALK WITH ME IN THIS PAIN. JUST TAKE IT AWAY." I was not ready to walk into His arms under these circumstances. I did not want Him to come any closer.

Stuffed down deep inside my humanity, I was subconsciously blaming the Lord for my anguish. At the same time, my faith heart was saying, *"All things work together for good to those who love the Lord."* The conflict was so great that it permeated every part of my life. I did not want to feel this way, but I felt trapped. My circumstances were not going to change and, at this point, praying about my emotions was not changing them, either.

Have you ever had an argument with your husband or wife, when your feelings were still hurting and your mate wanted to make up with you? He wanted a hug or a kiss, but you weren't ready for that. You wanted to grumble around a little longer or persuade him a little more to get your way? Well, I guess that is an illustration of my rebellious love and anger. The Lord had allowed so many heartaches and disappointments in my life that my heart was broken and I was not ready to fall into His arms. However, I still wanted him to hang around close by. If things got worse, I would really need him.

It was hard to go to church, especially seeing loving couples hold hands, sit with an arm around another, hearing their words of support in prayer and encouragement to each other in a group setting. I missed holding hands, as well as getting hugs. I longed for tender whispers and the physical presence of my sweetheart. These were all reminders of my loss. The feelings of envy I was experiencing were even more unsettling.

While in this state of anger, several things transpired. I was to walk a pathway to greater depths of health problems, along with deep-seated loneliness, anger, solitude and depression. I even became accident-prone and banged up two cars. I tried to drive through a closed metal garage door. I attended social activities to escape the depression, or spent hours on the golf course. It was good to have a short-lived feeling of light-heartedness. After all, wasn't it better to laugh than cry? It seemed easier to stuff the feelings that way. It was easier to laugh for a while, but when let-down time came, when the lock on the front door was turned to go into the empty house, depression returned, and loneliness was waiting on the other side of the door.

My medicine cabinet became a regular drug store filled with anything that would kill pain. However, I knew this was not the answer. My body seemed to be fighting this never-ending struggle as well. It wasn't long before I made two trips to the emergency room at nearby St. Jude Hospital. My blood pressure was at stroke level and the pains in my chest were almost unbearable. As a result, I was put on blood pressure medication and heart medication. I was told stress could be a killer. Was God going to take my health too? Was I going crazy? Death seemed like an easy way out. I really didn't want to live but I was too scared to do anything about it. Maybe God would intervene and just take me home to heaven in some natural way.

There was another transition of behavior that was beginning to happen. I did not want people around me. It was a comfort to be alone in my bedroom, but my family and friends would not let me isolate myself. More than once I did not have the privilege of saying, "No." My friend, Bonnie, had Monday night football dinners for a group of gals. Sometimes we ended up talking more than watching football. The boys and their families visited often and shared their lives which kept me in the land of the living. Lee and Gloria Bendell often invited me to their

Sunday School class at church and then to a weekly Care Group meeting. Never before had I witnessed the love of couples for a lone human being. This was so encouraging, especially in a world of twosomes.

There is another group of gals that have been a part of my life for years-my Bible study group on Tuesday mornings. Many times Bev Edwards would come to me and say, "You have been on my heart in prayer at the strangest times." Or different ones of the group would say they held me up in prayer and that they carried a heavy burden for me. Only a few have actually known the depth of my despair. I thank the Lord that He used these wonderful people to minister to my needs and, through them, I have seen His open arms waiting for me to run into them. God uses people to help people. It is God's way to show His love and to let us know that we are not alone. People are God's ambassadors who physically serve in His place. When they minister love one to another, it leaves its mark—God's mark.

Another feeling of turmoil was an attitude of self-condemnation. I was not only angry with the Lord for the trials, but I was angry with myself for having such a crummy attitude. Frankly, I was sick of all the introspection, the whining, and the feeling of anger itself. I could just picture the Lord carrying this overgrown, arm-and-leg-flying, immature adult/child down a long path. You know, like when your kids misbehaved in a restaurant and you took them outside (under pressure) to have a little talk. What a scene! However, the Lord was not doing that. He sent loving people around me and I felt Him quietly and lovingly waiting and understanding my emotions, my hurt.

Regardless of all of the feelings, I still knew He loved me as He always has.

Through my counselor, I was referred to a wonderful doctor who took time to listen. As I sat waiting in Dr. Sam Doolittle's office, he came through the door and said, "What's going on?" and "Let's talk." After relating the struggles, the run-away feelings and emotional stress caused by the events of my life, he was very understanding. After several tests, it seemed the blood pressure was the first thing to address. Dr. Dootlittle was kind and assured me life would get better. He said my negative feelings were normal for someone in depression, but I had to understand that it would take patience, time and medical help. It was such a relief to talk to someone about the things that had been tearing me apart. He assured me there was hope and help. I was a classic case of depression. To me that sounded like something a Christian should not have, but Dr. Dootlittle was sincere and so was I. I was in depression! It was then that I started my research on the subject of depression, its effects, and the therapy for healing.

The book *Coping With Depression*[1] was recommended. It was so fascinating to follow my progress in the depression as I read the book. Dr. Archibald Hart, Ph. D. mentions seven stages of depression:

1. Self-Condemnation
2. Guilt feelings
3. Boredom and spiritual emptiness

---

[1] *Coping With Depression*; Archibald D. Hart, Ph.D.; © 1994 by Word, Inc., Waco, Texas.

4. Anger
5. Fatigue and weakness
6. Slowed thinking and poor memory
7. Delusions

So far I had hit all seven.

As the weeks went by, I spent hours in the Scriptures. I copied down every promise that I came across that pertained to God's love and strength for me. These verses were put on Rolodex cards for easy access and constant referral. The process of healing was beginning.

> *"O Lord, you have examined my heart and know everything about me. You know when I sit or stand. When far away you know my every thought. You chart the path ahead of me and tell me where to stop and rest. Every moment you know where I am. You know what I am going to say before I even say it. You both precede and follow me and place your hand of blessing on my head"* (Psalm 139:1-5 LB).

> *"But we have this treasure in earthen vessels, that the surpassing greatness of the power may be of God, and not of us. We are troubled on every side, yet not distressed; we are perplexed, but not in despair; Persecuted, but not forsaken; cast down, but not destroyed"* (II Cor. 4:7-9 KJV).

> *"When you pass through the waters, I will be with you, and through the rivers, they shall not overflow you. When you walk through the fire, you shall not be scorched"* (Isa. 43:2 NAS).

> *"Even when we are too weak to have any faith left, he remains faithful to us and will help us, for he cannot disown us who are a part of himself, and he will always carry out his promises to us"* (II Tim. 2:13 LB).

It takes serenity, courage and wisdom to maintain a healthy attitude when life isn't fair, We can't change the fact that our world is imperfect, and that things are far from the way we think they should be, but we can choose the attitude we will take. We need serenity from God to change our response to the injustices of life. We need courage to face with optimism the days when we were treated unfairly. We need wisdom to know whether to fight injustice or to make the best of a bad situation.[2]

Serenity means to be calm and unruffled, peaceful, placid, tranquil, unperturbed.

Courage means mental or moral strength to venture, persevere, and withstand danger, fear, or difficulty.

Wisdom means an ability to discern inequalities and relationships; insights.[3]

"We don't always have to be strong or pretend to be perfect. We can live a real life, with daily struggles, in a human body beset with weakness, and still find the power

---

[2] *The Life Recovery Bible*, © 1992, Tyndale House Publishers, Inc., Wheaton, IL 60189.
[3] Merriam-Webster Collegiate Dictionary, tenth edition, © 1996, Springfield, Massachusetts.

from above to keep going without being crushed and broken."[4]

The Lord's idea of brokenness may be different than mine, I thought, but I would give it my best shot. To be a well and productive Christian was a goal to reach for. Besides that, the Lord uses a lot of broken things. Maybe He could still use my life to bring glory His name. This was definitely a wilderness jourey, but He knows all about that too.

---

[4] *The Life Recovery Bible Notes*, © 1998, Steven Atterburn and David Stoop; published in association with the Literary Agency of Alive Communications, Inc., 1465 Kelly Johnson Blvd., Colorado Springs, CO 80920, p. 1395.

Chapter Sixteen

The Will of God?

OTHERS

Dedicated to our Marcie who always thought of others. She gave joy to others and was always ready to give a smile or a hug.

A compliment or a pat on the back,
Or praise with a kind word to give,
Makes a person want to do their best,
And really want to live.

It isn't the things that cost a lot,
That provide true joy in the heart.
No, it's the simple things like a smile or a hug,
Free—and easy to impart.

Duane D. Logsdon

Chapter 16

THE WILL OF GOD?

What a fun morning! As I parked the golf cart in the carport, I felt tired but it was a good kind of tiredness. Being in the desert to watch the sunrise and to play golf with special friends was a privilege. The morning had been spent on a good golf game and the laughter that accompanied the golf made the soul merry. It was good to be back home though, besides that I was getting hungry. As I walked through the door, Mother greeted me with a statement that made my heart hit the floor.

"Honey, you are to call your sister-in-law, Carol. There has been a family tragedy, She wanted you to call her as soon as you got in."

Stopping dead in my tracks all kinds of thoughts flashed through my mind.

Who?

What?

When?

Where?

How?

As I picked up the telephone receiver, it felt like dead weight. My fingers stumbled over the numbers and I had to make several tries at dialing her number. "Carol, you called? What happened?"

In the past months, I had experienced the pain of losing my loved ones in death ... slowly. There had been time to pray about the loss before it happened. There had been time to try to get used to the feeling that my loved ones would be leaving for their home in heaven. It's true, however, that even though you know the inevitable will happen, you can never really prepare yourself.

None-the-less, no one is ready for a suicide. The pain is wrenching. The shock is stunning. The hurt is deep. For seconds you lose contact with reality. Unbelief takes over the mind. Then the tears start to flow.

There was a long silence for both of us before Carol told the story.

It was our niece, Marcie. She had taken her life early that morning.

My heart hurt for my family—for Margie, Marcie's mother, and Don, her stepfather. What must they be going through?

Already tentative plans were being discussed for the funeral. On top of this tragedy, the Carolina's were being bit with the worst snowstorm in years. Airports were closed, people were stranded and planes were grounded. Would it be possible for any of us even to get to North Carolina?

I have mentioned Marcie's name earlier in this book as our niece who took her girl friend with us on family vacations. The girl friend would later become our daughter-in-law. When Marcie was younger, we had close times and fun times. After she grew up and married, we did not see her often but still, we kept in touch.

Marcie was a child who loved life. She was cute, spirited and a lot of fun. She gave us lots of laughs and I can remember her at two years of age dancing around the living room with a lamp shade on her head, The more we laughed the more she put into the show. Her laughter was infectious.

When Marcie was a child, she gave her heart to the Lord and accepted Him as her personal Savior. After her first marriage, she spent several years doing missionary work in Scotland. In the course of her life, she lost four full-term babies and had several miscarriages. Because of the trauma, her first marriage broke up and she went into a deep depression that required psychiatric care. After several years of being single, she regained her health, remarried and had a lovely daughter. Again she started having pressures in life and in her home, She went through another bout of depression and Margie and Don eventually took Marcie into their home where she had lived for the past year-and-a-half.

Even through her struggle with disappointment and depression, her life was filled with love for her family and friends. Life was not easy for Marcie but she again struggled back to health enough to take a job. She met new friends and she was active in her church, witnessing for the Lord whenever she could. In fact, in Marcie's mind, life was becoming normal again and (not mentioning it to her family) she had taken herself off her medication for about six months. Two weeks before her death, her family noticed many behavioral changes, so Margie and Don took her to the psychiatrist. She was put back on medication.

This time Marcie would not recover.

There were questions in my mind about mental illness, depression and suicide. Trying to reason this all out in my mind became confusing. Until we have to face it, we know little about the different kinds of depression and the effects they produce in people's lives.

When thinking through my niece's tragic suicide, I contacted Dr. Clyde Narramore, pioneer in the field of Christian psychology and founder of the Narramore Christian Foundation. He shared a great deal of information which was helpful. Here are some of his insights:

Why people commit suicide: There are many reasons why a person may feel life is no longer worth living. Naturally, the reasons vary from person to person. But if you were to study the cases of a thousand or more who have committed suicide, you would often find the following reasons:

1. Facing a seemingly intolerable situation: A person who has lost all hope may feel there is no way out, that he has reached a situation for which there is no answer. A family member or a friend may look at the situation and see how a problem could be solved and wonder why the suicide victim felt the way he or she did, but, of course, he did not have the same emotional dynamics nor did the suicide victim feel that he had any resources. He felt he was in a condition that had no solution.
2. Desiring to punish or get even with survivors: A person who is functioning normally may think it strange that anyone would choose suicide to punish another person. But such is the case in many instances. A victim may have unbearable strong feelings against a person or persons and may want to get even and punish them, so

he chooses his ultimate weapon of sacrifice— death. Instead of striking out at others or confronting them, he turns his feelings inward and in a sense says, "They'll be sorry for what they've done when they find that I've taken my life. I'll get even with them." Such a person has usually not learned to confront others or to work through difficult issues. Consequently, he or she resorts to taking his own life. This may occur more frequently among inexperienced young people than with those who are older and more mature.

3. Wanting to avoid being a burden: Many people who take their lives or who have thought often about suicide feel they are not contributing to society or to their family. So they begin to feel that taking their life is the ultimate solution to no longer being a burden to those who have to take care of them, finance them, and do for them what they no longer can do for themselves. They look back on their active days and feel they are nothing but a burden.

4. Desiring to join a deceased person: A person may irrationally believe that if he could just die he would somehow be reunited with someone he has lost. He may erroneously believe that reuniting with someone who has passed away will make him feel better, more secure, protected, less lonely and better understood. So he takes his own life, not understanding that death does not necessarily bring about a future companionship.

5. Having nothing to live for: Some people during irrational states feel they have no value unless they are doing something for themslves or for other people. Their value and worth is entwined with "doing." When

they reach a point when they are no longer contributing, they believe there is no reason to remain on earth. They usually do not have a close relationship with Christ.

6. Avoiding severe suffering: Pain is a terrible thing, especially when it is severe and relentless. A person may suffer to the extent that he feels he can never have relief from extreme pain. He may have medical and other types of help, but still the pain keeps destroying his world. So in an attempt to obtain relief, he takes steps to end it all through suicide.

7. Being deeply depressed: A person who has never experienced severe depression may not understand the utter feelings of hopelessness that depression brings. One who is deeply depressed most of the time may feel that he is in a deep hole with no way out. To make it worse, his acquaintances may blithely say, "You've got to pull yourself together," or, "Just snap out of it!" Such statements tell the suicidal person that they do not understand and cannot possibly help.

8. Feelings that no one understand or cares: When a person has suicidal feelings he may come to believe that no one really understands or even cares how he feels. In fact, "friends" may have told him that they just can't understand him. These remarks are often followed by walking away from the suffering person. In his frustration, the so-called friend realizes that whatever he has said or done hasn't helped, so he avoids the suffering person. This (to the sufferer) proves his suspicion that no one really cares.

9. Believing that death is the end and that a person no longer has consciousness or feelings: Many people

don't understand God's eternal Word, and may erroneously believe that death ends it all. They do not realize that God clearly said in His holy Word, *"For it is appointed unto man once to die, and after that the judgment"* (Hebrews 9:27). He may not understand that the soul will live on for all eternity either separated from God or living joyously in His wonderful presence. Since he is not biblically taught, he may feel that the fastest way to escape pain and torment is suicide.

These, then, are some of the reasons why people consider suicide. They also suggest what a loved one or family member can do to help the suicidal person before it is too late.

1. Signs that an adult or teenager may be contemplating taking his own life:
    a. Frequent work or school absences, or doing poor daily work.
    b. Negative talk about bosses or teachers or others in authority.
    c. Withdrawal—preferring to be alone rather than enjoying the company of others.
    d. Little or no interest in spiritual matters. No longer participating in church activities, Bible reading and prayer.
    e. Having times of moodiness and being continually downhearted and sad. Showing signs of depression.
    f. Being uncommunicative, not wanting to talk or socialize or joke with others; remaining quiet and non-talkative.

g. Changes in eating and sleeping habits. A person may want to overeat or on the other hand, not to eat at all. He may want to sleep nearly all of the time or on the contrary, he may be unable to sleep regularly.
h. Giving away prized possessions. Some people before taking their lives see to it that friends receive some of the possessions which mean so much to them.
i. Unusual irritation and anger. A person who is considering suicide may become upset about minor things and may be unduly angry much of the time.
j. Consuming alcohol or other drugs. A person with suicidal feelings may turn to drinking and using dangerous drugs.
k. Preoccupation with death and dying. Before committing suicide a person may talk a great deal about death. He may be reading morbid articles or watching TV or internet programs having to do with dying. In other words, he is identifying with death.
l. Threatening to take one's life. Although many people who threaten to take their lives never carry through, friends should not dismiss the seriousness of such statements. Most people who take their lives have indeed made threats about it. Consequently, such statements should not be overlooked or minimized.

2. Conditions frequently associated with increased risk of suicide:
   a. Divorce, separation, broken relations, stress with the family.
   b. Loss of job, home, money, status, self-esteem, or personal security.

c. Loss of health (real or imaginary).
d. Death or terminal illness of a relative or friend.
e. Depression, bi-polar disorder.
f. Alcohol or drug abuse.
g. No dynamic faith in God, being unsaved.

3. Suicide and Salvation:

People often ask me if a person who commits suicide is able to go to heaven. The answer is yes, because salvation is not earned by what a person does. Rather, salvation depends on what Christ has already done. A person in an irrational state of mind will believe almost anything, but salvation and eternal life are based upon Christ and His death on Calvary's cross, coupled with a person's acceptance of Christ's death as an atonement or covering for his sins. John 3:16 says, *"For God so loved the world that He gave His only son, that whosoever believes in Him should not perish but have everlasting life."*

The permanence of a person's salvation is highlighted in many portions of Scripture such as John 10:28: *"And I give unto them eternal life, and they shall never perish; neither shall anyone snatch them out of My hand."*

One of the strongest portions of Scripture dealing with our relationship with Christ is Romans 8:38-39: *"For I am persuaded that neither death nor life, nor angels nor principalities nor power, nor things present nor things to come, nor height nor depth, nor any other created thing, shall be able to separate us from the love of God which is in Christ Jesus our Lord."* Notice that this Scripture includes suicide.

Feelings at the time of suicide may be extreme and irrational, but they do not determine ones' salvation.

4. Bipolar Disorder:

For many years, we have heard about a serious disorder called manic depression. It is described as severe mood swings, sometimes with deep depression, and other times with feelings of elation, euphoria and joy.

In recent years, this manic-depressive condition has been referred to as a BIPOLAR DISORDER. It is characterized by moods that swing in two opposite poles or directions—mania (mood elevation) to depression.

In discussing tendencies toward self-destruction, it is important to consider bipolar disorders, because a person who is in a severe mood depression may feel that life is not worth living. The symptoms of depression in a bipolar disorder are almost identical to those of major depression. They may include moods of feeling sad, fatigue or loss of energy, insomnia, excessive sleeping, weight gains or loss, diminished ability to concentrate or make decisions, feelings of guilt, pessimism, helplessness, and low self-esteem. These severe episodes of depression vary from person to person, but they may last as much as six to twelve months at a time.

Professionals who study bipolar disorders believe there is no single cause for it. Instead, a combination of biologic, genetic, and environmental factors tend to trigger and perpetuate this complex disorder.

This illness is of great importance since it is estimated that 15 to 20 per cent of those who suffer from bipolar disorder and who do not receive medical attention, commit suicide. Consequently, it is imperative that those who suffer from this disorder receive medical attention, as well as psychological counseling. A person may go for years suffering from this disorder yet not seek help. Also, family members may minimize the problem feeling that the victim is just "in a bad mood."

Treatments for the condition are usually focused on reducing the frequency, severity, as well as the social and psychological consequences. Therapists, of course, are eager to see that the victim is functioning as effectively as possible during such episodes. The condition is not limited only to adults. Children, too, may be affected by bipolar disorders.

Following are several references that may be helpful to better understand bipolar disorder:

The Narramore Christian Foundation has published a booklet written by Dr. Todd W. Hall, Ph.D., entitled, Understanding Bipolar Disorder. It is available free of charge by phoning the Foundation at 1(800)477-5893, or writing to P. O. Box 661900, Arcadia, CA 91066-1900.

Another very helpful book by Dr. Kay Redfield Jamison is *An Unquiet Mind*, available at nearly all bookstores. Dr. Redfield, herself suffering from a bipolar disorder, is a psychiatrist. Although the book is not written from a Christian background, it is one of the most helpful books on this disorder available today.

Chapter Seventeen

Tried and True

TRUE SUCCESS

So you'd like to be successful,
And make it big some day?
There's nothing wrong with that desire
When motives are okay.

But making money just to be rich,
Isn't really true success.
In fact, riches in themselves
Can make your life a mess.

Deception comes when we are told
Money brings all we pray,
That's only true if in your plans,
You want it to give away.

There's a mystery that's God's design
The purpose for which we live,
True fulfillment and success,
Is not to keep, but to give.

So you'd like to be successful,
And make it big some day?
Then keep only what you need,
And give the rest away.

Chapter 17

TRIED AND TRUE

It was nearly midnight, December 31, 1999. Another year had passed and as usual it was time for serious thinking and to evaluate the experiences of the past year, or years. It was a time to be honest about victories, failures, hard places, and to thank my Lord for his love, care and faithfulness. It was a time to evaluate my spiritual progress and to set goals for the coming year.

Frankly, I felt like a lump of wet clay in the Potter's hands. I had no aspirations to be anything, or to be any kind of vessel except that for which He intended. The outward appearance did not matter as long as I was in His will, doing what He wanted me to do.

I asked the Lord for **honesty** to evaluate the past, for **hope** to continue my journey, **strength** to endure and to have **single vision and clarity** to love Him and trust Him beyond the capabilities of my humanity. Is this asking too much? I think not as I look back at how He has unraveled all the loss and pain for my good.

As I sat on the couch, facing my desk and the glass-fronted shelf above it, my eyes focused on an object that at one time represented a totally disastrous event. Now it was only a reminder of God's faithfulness. Maybe this was why it was purchased in the first place. It was something that proved Romans 8:28 to be "Tried and True":

"And we know that God causes
all things to work together for good
to those who love God,
to those who are called
according to His purpose" (NAS).

The object of my gaze was a sealed glass dome filled with shredded pieces of real money that at one time had been worth $1,000,000.00.

My mind flashed back to Duane's involvement as a board member for a new bank in Orange County, California. This was a new experience in teaming, an opportunity to meet new friends and business acquaintances. It began when a local businessman contacted Duane on two different occasions while we were on vacation. Duane's argument was that he was already involved as founding chairman of the Luis Palau Evangelistic Team and had been for several years. He also stated that he was on the boards of the Narramore Christian Foundation and Whittier Christian High School. The caller confided that Duane's involvement would be an asset to the new bank as well as giving him contacts for the organizations he represented. Besides that, he would not have to be present at all of the meetings. After several days, we felt we had backed this up with much prayer and the motives seemed right so Duane returned the call and accepted the responsibility.

Life seemed to be rocking along in a very pleasant manner when Duane had to have minor repair surgery. I was just finishing a two-year medical assistant training course when he went in for the surgery. So, with study books in hand, I made my way to see Duane at Long Beach

Memorial Hospital before his surgery. The nurse came in to give him his pre-op injection and left the room. Almost immediately, Duane said, "I am so sick." Looking up, I realized he was going into anaphylactic shock, so I ran to the nurses' station for help. A "Code Blue" was announced over the public address system and people converged from everywhere. Duane responded well enough to go on with the surgery a few hours later. Little did we know that this same thing would happen again about a year-and-a-half later (same surgery, different pre-op injection). This time the trauma came post-operative in the recovery room and later again in his hospital room. It was then that we realized that he was allergic to most narcotic drugs. It was after this experience and during Duane's recovery that a call came from a friend saying the bank was "in trouble." Duane was too ill with the after-effects and damage done to his nervous system to even discuss the situation. I called close friends to start a prayer chain about this matter and to keep praying. I didn't know what else to do.

Several weeks passed before Duane became really aware of the seriousness of the problem. He talked with several bank board members and tried to get to the bottom of the problem and to come up with some solution to help protect those who had made investments. In the process of all this, Duane had a relapse and was confined to bed and constant medical care. It seemed the added stress on top of the nervous system trauma he was suffering was causing a nervous breakdown.

As the bank went into more difficulty, three of the board members tried to solve the problem by infusing capital in return for notes that would repay their investment. Collateral was put up but the new bank did not respond with good notes. After the FDIC came into the picture, several lists were discovered showing where some of the bank officers had revised the lists to our disadvantage. As a result, the three people who put up the money lost homes, businesses and capital. To us, this was a personal $750,000 loss. To my knowledge some of these people never recovered their money. We felt bad that our friends had lost their investments.

It was through this experience that attorney, Susan Medwied, became my constant companion. Sitting in for Duane at bank board meetings, I needed her constant advice and wisdom. She is the type of lawyer you want on your side of the table and not across the table from you. She delved into many corporate situations and became our legal representative to the very end. I will be forever grateful to her. Needless to say, I learned a lot about banking ... and people.

After seeing Duane's name on the front pages of the business section of the *L.A. Times* and the *Orange County Register*, we couldn't help but wonder what the Lord was doing with our lives. Was the decision to get involved in the bank an opportunity, or a disaster that was brought on by a big "ego" trip? We were at a crossroads regarding how important money was to us anyway. We had peace about trying to help and felt we had done the right thing. If the Lord provided the money in the first place, He would know how to replace it or use it however He saw fit. We felt like Job when he said, "*But he knoweth the way that I take, when he hath tried me, I shall come forth as gold.*"

Someone once said, "Godly men can do without wealth, but wealthy men cannot do without God." I found an old Chinese proverb in the book, *More Precious Than Gold* by Lottie Beth Hobb (a study on Job):

"God is tested by fire, man by gold."[1]

We prayed more about our attitude regarding losing the money than we did about recovering the loss. Our priority was to stay in love with the Lord and we did not want this loss to mar our fellowship with Him.

Susan continued her involvement in legal matters with us, going to meetings and working through stacks of paper. A few years later, she called and said, "The case is closed, the files are stored and it is all over." I put the glass dome filled with shreds of money on a high shelf and forgot about it. That was until New Year's Eve, 1999. In fact, I remember very few of the names of the people involved. I do remember though how the Lord answered our prayers.

Nothing is impossible with God! We were able to use the loss through the years as an income tax write-off and the Lord provided through other investments to make up the difference. I also should add that our commitment to tithe was still honored because His shovel is always bigger than ours. Where there is a will, He will provide the way.

I had great hope for year 2000 despite not having Duane at my side. God alone can turn our tragedies into triumphs! He can take the tragedy of divorce, death and all of the feelings of emotional pain and loss and work them all out for His honor and glory. I didn't know how He would

---

[1] *More Precious Than Gold*, Lottie Beth Hobb; © 1969 Harvest Publications, PO Box 3304, Fort Worth, TX 76105.

do that for me, but my prayer was that I would be found faithful in season and out of season with what He has entrusted to my care.

Since the very first New Year I celebrated after becoming a child of God, my spiritual mother (Mrs. Grace Yaxley) instilled into me for every New Year's planning, the use of a random selection of a New Year's Bible verse. With my promise box of verses in hand, and a prayer on my lips, I asked the Lord to give me the verse He wanted me to have for that year. It was Isaiah 45:2-3 (LB):

"I will go before you, and level the mountains
and smash down the city gates of brass and iron bars,

And I will give you ***treasures hidden in darkness,***

secret riches;

and you will know that I am doing this,

the Lord God of Israel,
the one who calls you by your name."

Chapter Eighteen

Miracle of the Heart

THE EYES OF THE HEART

You say you see it, but you don't,
Yet you still believe.
The Bible calls this the gift of faith,
Which your eyes cannot perceive.

Faith comes by believing the Word of God,
That what It says is true.
With your mind and heart you choose to believe,
Then It really becomes part of you.

It shapes your thoughts and impacts your life,
And it shows you how to live.
When this is true, attention to
It's principles and values you'll give.

The Bible teaches you how to live,
It teaches you how to die.
It assures you that you can be Heaven-bound,
But we can't do it alone if we try.

Yes, I can say that I see it,
And I've experienced that it's true.
With my vision I may not see this faith,
But with the eyes of my heart, I do.

Duane D. Logsdon

Chapter 18

MIRACLE OF THE HEART

Grief is a journey. It takes us down a path of feelings and emotions that are bewildering. As Christians, it is a journey that we walk alone with God. Our personality differences make our personal experience unique, different from anyone else's. Studies have shown that there are stages in the grieving process but there is no set order in that process.

"The early stage is one of unfeeling shock, when everything seems to engulf the griever in wraps of numbness and contradiction and inability to concentrate. Disbelief, rebellion, weariness, and irrational behavior are all symptoms of grief. Few are prepared for the actual chest pain and the sense of anxiety which grief often causes."[1]

Archibald Hart says: "Where a legitimate loss has occurred, the process of grieving must be fully implemented; the depressed person must be given every opportunity to mourn the loss. Such grief, when it is allowed, is normal, natural, and self-limiting. It can help for close friends to give clear 'permission' for the depressed person to grieve. This can be done either verbally or by an attitude of acceptance. If a person who has suffered the loss

---

[1] *After The Flowers Are Gone*; Bea Decker as told by Gladys Kooiman; © 1972; The Zondervan Corp., Grand Rapids, Mich.

wants to be alone, avoid responsibility, and back down from previous commitments, this should be allowed; *grieving cannot take place in the midst of activity.* The right attitude of acceptance and unconditional love—observing the wishes of the sufferer, giving him "space" if he wants it, refraining from pressuring him—can make the difference between a 'normal' depression and one that will be painfully prolonged. It is particularly important to reassure the sufferer that the depression is not outside God's will for him or her, that it is not a sign of failure or of God's rejection."[2]

I'm so glad that my family and friends allowed me this kind of understanding, love and freedom. I'm glad the Lord understands our humanity and frailty. Psalm 103:14 says, "*For he himself knows our frame; he is mindful that we are but dust.*"

Grief is not only a journey, it is a form of suffering that at some time in our life we all will experience. We can go through many types of suffering. There is persecution because of our faith in Jesus Christ, and there is suffering we bring on ourselves because of sin, as well as physical and spiritual suffering.

Grief is an emotional suffering caused by severe loss. What are some of the reasons for these trials?

> "*After you have suffered for a little the God of all grace, who has called you to his eternal glory in Christ, will himself,* ***perfect, confirm and establish you***" (I Peter 5:10).

---

[2] *Coping With Depression*; Archibald Hart; © 1984; Word Publisher; Waco, Texas.

Elizabeth Elliot, in her book, *The Path Of Loneliness*, speaks of this process: "There are many things that God does not fix—precisely **because** He loves us. Instead of extracting us from the problem, He calls on us to stand fast. In our sorrow or loneliness or pain, **He** calls..."[3] The Lord wants to "perfect" us; that is, He wants to bring us to spiritual maturity—to conform us to His image and establish us in our faith walk and relationship with Him.

Life's experiences are the tools that he uses to prepare us for eternity.

> "*What a wonderful God we have—he is the Father of our Lord Jesus Christ, the source of every mercy, and the one who so wonderfully comforts and strengthens us in our hardships and trials. And why does he do this? So that when others are troubled, needing our sympathy and encouragement,* ***we can pass on to them this same help and comfort*** *God has given us*" (II Cor. 1:3,4 LB).

We are to share with others who need our sympathy and encouragement. We are to share with others the comfort and hope God has given us in our time of need.

He has promised us:

1. **His strength:** "*I can do all things through Christ who strengthens me*" (Phil. 4:13).

---

[3] *The Path Of Loneliness*; Elizabeth Elliot; © 1988; Oliver-Nelson Books, a division of Thomas Nelson, Inc., Nashville, Tennessee.

2. **His faithfulness:** "*He who calls you* (to a task or into a situation, etc.) *is faithful, and he will do it*" (I Thess. 5:24).

3. **His stability:** "*And he shall be the stability (or faithfulness) of your times...*" (Isa. 33:6).

Grief is also an experience of personal growth in who we are and where we are in our spiritual journey. Sometimes the Word is very clear in revealing our true condition. One of the verses that has changed my thinking process in grief and loss is:

> "*He died for all, that they who live should no longer live for themselves, but for him who died and rose again on their behalf*" (II Cor. 5:15).

There is a note in my Bible beside that verse that says, "REDEMPTION FROM SELF-CENTEREDNESS." When going through the grief process, we can become so preoccupied with ourselves that we lose sight of the bigger picture—the lessons God wants us to learn—the lessons that make Him our "ALL"—the lessons that have eternal value.

After receiving medical help, my mental attitude and outlook on life changed very rapidly. Life became more tolerable and the interpersonal relationships in my life became a joy. I could hardly wait to be in church or with my family and friends. I had a desire to help others that I did not have before. I do not believe this was totally due to the medication, but that helped. I also believe my grief period was coming to an end and God was performing a miracle in my heart to thank Him and praise Him not only for being with me but for being with Duane as well.

This book is the story of the struggles with life, death, loss and change for both of us. The last Christmas we had together, Duane got out of bed, put on his robe (he was very ill at the time), and made his way down the stairs. He held in his hand the last Christmas gift he would give me. In that little gift-wrapped box was a silver and gold heart necklace. On the back of that necklace was the poem "Footprints." I cherish that necklace and the poem. Its words and its truth are our testimony.

FOOTPRINTS

One night a man had a dream.
He was walking along the beach with the Lord
and across the sky flashed scenes from his life.
In each scene, he noticed two sets of footprints in the sand;
one made by him, and the other by the Lord.
When the last scene of his life flashed before him,
he looked back at the footprints in the sand.
He noticed that many times along the path of his life
there was only one set of footprints. He also noticed
that it happened at the worst times in his life.
This bothered him very much, so he asked the Lord about it.
"Lord, You said that once I decided to follow You,
You'd walk with me all the way.
But I've noticed that during times of trouble,
there is only one set of footprints.
I don't understand why You left me
when I needed You the most."
The Lord answered, "My precious child, I love you
and I would never leave you.
During your times of trial,
when you see only one set of footprints,
that's when I was carrying you."

\- M. R. Powers

Chapter Nineteen

Treasures Hidden in the Darkness

Chapter 19

TREASURES IN THE DARKNESS

And He will be the stability of your times, A wealth of salvation, wisdom and knowledge; the fear of the Lord is his treasure (Isa.33:6 NAS).

[He is] the God who made both earth and heaven, the seas and everything in them. He is God who keeps every promise, who gives justice to the poor and oppressed and food to the hungry. He frees the prisoners and opens the eyes of the blind; he lifts the burdens from those bent down beneath their loads. For the Lord loves good men. He protects the immigrants and cares for the orphans and widows. But he turns topsy-turvy the plans of the wicked (Psalm 146:6-9 LB).

No, I will not abandon you or leave you as orphans in the storm—I will come to you (John 14:18 LB).

Yet what we suffer now is nothing compared to the glory he will give us later (Rom. 8:18 LB).

Where is the man who fears the Lord? God will teach him how to choose the best. He will live within God's circle of blessing and his children shall inherit the earth. Friendship with God is reserved for those who reverence him. With them alone he shares the secrets of his promises (Psalm 25:12-14 LB).

But in our trouble God has comforted us—and this, too, to help you; to show you from personal experience how God will tenderly comfort you when you undergo these same sufferings. He will give you the strength to endure (II Cor. 1: 7-8 LB).

Lord, when doubts fill my mind, when my heart is in turmoil, quiet me and give me renewed hope and cheer (Psalm 94:19 LB).

What a wonderful God we have—he is the Father of our Lord Jesus Christ, the source of every mercy, and the one who so wonderfully comforts and strengthens us in our hardships and trials. Why does he do this? So that when others are troubled, needing our sympathy and encouragement, we can pass on to them this same help and comfort God has given us (II Cor. 1: 3-4 LB).

But they that wait upon the Lord shall renew their strength. They shall mount up with wings like eagles; they shall run and not be weary; they shall walk and not faint (Isa.40:31 LB).

Happy, are those who are strong in the Lord, who want above all else to follow your steps. When they walk through the Valley of Weeping, it will become a place of springs where pools of blessings and refreshment collect after rains! (Psalm 84:5 LB).

Jehovah himself is caring for you! He is your defender. He protects you day and night. He keeps you from all evil and preserves your life. He keeps his eye upon you as you come and go and always guards you (Psalm 121:5-8 LB).

You are my hiding place from every storm of life; you even keep me from getting into trouble! You surround me with songs of victory. I will instruct you (says the Lord) and guide you along the best pathway for your life; I will advise you and watch your progress (Psalm 32:7-8 LB).

You have seen me tossing and turning through the night. You have collected all my tears and preserved them in your bottle! You have recorded every one in your book (Psalm 56:8 LB).

To all those who mourn...he will give: beauty for ashes; joy instead of mourning; praise instead of heaviness (Isa. 61:3 LB).

God is our refuge and strength. a tested help in times of trouble (Psalm 46:1 LB).

...by our faith -- the Holy Spirit helps us with our daily problems and in our praying For we don't even know what we should pray for nor how to pray as we should, but the Holy Spirit prays for us with such feeling that it cannot be expressed in words. And the Father who knows all hearts knows, of course, what the Spirit is saying as he pleads for us in harmony with God's own will. And we know that all that happens to us is working for our good if we love God and are fitting into his plans (Romans 8:26-28 LB).

He heals the brokenhearted, binding up their wounds (Psalm 147:3 LB).

We live within the shadow of the Almighty, sheltered by the God who is above all gods. This I declare, that he alone is my refuge, my place of safety; he is my God, and I am trusting him (Psalm 91:1-2 LB).

For he himself knows our frame; he is mindful that we are but dust (Psalm 103:14 LB).

The Lord is close to those whose hearts are breaking; he rescues those who are humbly sorry for their sins. The good man does not escape all troubles—he has them too. But the Lord helps him in each and every one (Psalm 34:18.19 LB).

...the sorrows of widowhood will be remembered no more, for your Creator will be your "husband." The Lord Almighty is his name; he is your redeemer, the Holy One of Israel, the God of all the earth. For the Lord has called you back from your grief (Isa. 54:4-6 LB).